T0248152

Romanticise Your Life

Romanticise Your Life

How to Find Romance & Joy in the Everyday

BETH McCOLL

First published in Great Britian in 2024 by Orion Spring,
an imprint of The Orion Publishing Group Ltd
Carmelite House, 50 Victoria Embankment
London EC4Y 0DZ

An Hachette UK Company

1 3 5 7 9 10 8 6 4 2

A CIP catalogue record for this book is available from the British Library.

ISBN (Hardback) 978 1 3987 2086 2
ISBN (eBook) 978 1 3987 2087 9
ISBN (Audio) 978 1 3987 2088 6

Quote on p.19 from 'Summer in a Small Town' from the collection
Unincorporated Persons in Late Honda Dynasty published by Graywolf Press.
Copyright © Tony Hoagland 2010.

Designed by Goldust Design
Printed and bound in Great Britain by Clays Ltd, Elcograf S.p.A
Illustrations by Saskia Leboff

www.orionbooks.co.uk

For Jackie.

Contents

Contents

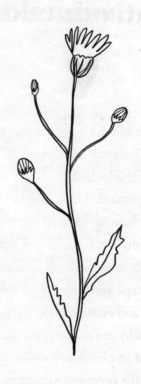

Introduction

Romanticise your life. It's a phrase you've probably seen more and more over the last few years – perhaps as a brand slogan or article headline or beneath a snap on social media accompanied by a long caption about reinventing yourself, buying yourself nice things, behaving as though your life is a film. Maybe you thought there was something to it, something you might want to try yourself. Or perhaps you rolled your eyes, dismissing it as self-indulgent and even outright delusional.

It's easy to see why you might immediately write off the idea. We're taught in childhood to use our imaginations and then later, at the precipice of joining the adult world, we're taught to discard them. There's a brief time to play, to imagine, to think outside of the box, to indulge our dreams. As quickly as that time arrives it has passed; those skills are packed away, exchanged for practicality, pragmatism and a smaller, more ordinary view of everything. We are told to put down childish fancies and enter early adulthood – a land of duty and work, forging a career, paying off loans, navigating relationships and handling many new and difficult responsibilities. It's understandable, then, that this might dent a person's ability to see the romance and joy in life, or to feel curious or excited or playful.

I felt this myself when I entered my twenties. I was depressed and anxious, unsure of which direction to take but certain that all the moves I was making were the wrong ones. I looked at myself and saw only what I lacked or was struggling with, the things I believed I couldn't have or be. I told myself that my dreams of a bigger life had been childish, nothing more than a trick I had played on myself. From beneath my stress and my misery, I deduced that real life couldn't be romantic. It could only ever be more of the same – a slog from one deadline to another, one hard day to the next. It was obligation and difficulty with only small moments of joy.

Unsurprisingly, this kind of thinking shut me off from so much of the available romance and magic of life. When my depression was at its deepest, I lost touch with my imagination, a place that had once represented pure opportunity and bliss. I was intimidated and over-whelmed, battling with demons and bad days that seemed at times to be insurmountable. And so, for a while, I decided that the best way to live was to keep my head down and just endure, giving most of what I had to other people and keeping very little for myself.

Sadly, I don't think this is unusual. Many of us live like this at one time or another, just placing one foot in front of the other, treating joy and play as something meant for other people. Many of us wait for our lives to become beautiful and good without our own input or say so, hoping for a miracle in the shape of somebody else, a person who will arrive as if out of a dream to give us the permission we've been waiting for to be playful, earnest, honest, brave and romantic.

This doesn't happen, of course.

It doesn't work like that.

There is no magical saviour; there is only us with our hearts and our hands and our thawing imaginations. It is us who must do the work of lifting ourselves out of these small and meek ways of living to make things better, bigger and more romantic. It is us who must build new and better philosophies around pleasure and romance, joy and indulgence. It is us who must open the shutters and let the light in, unlearning and then relearning, pulling up those old and tired beliefs at their roots – beliefs about how a person should live, what they deserve, what is embarrassing, what is not.

Doing this takes time but I promise that it is time you have. On the other side of this work can be a confidence and a self-assuredness that is like a cold glass of water in a heatwave. It's a sense of yourself and the world that makes it so much easier to be here. It's the knowledge that you are allowed to find what is beautiful and then go towards it without hesitating. It might seem frivolous to some people, and that's fine. In fact, there can be power in acknowledging other people's disapproval and judgement and then letting that go. After all, pleasing strangers was never your job; your only job is to try to live a life that feels good and is tailored for you. You will find your own ability to choose – to some degree at least – how it feels to be here, to live, to move over the earth.

To make something romantic is to make it better, softer and sweeter. It is to take a step beyond where you have been told all your life the limit is. Romanticising your life means going towards the places where your heart is pointing, even when doing this makes you feel so vulnerable that you think you might shatter or that your heart will crawl up out of your mouth and make a break for it. Romanticising your life means enduring this discomfort, sitting with it and calmly waiting for it to pass, while trusting and knowing that it always will. It is deciding that your own desires and daydreams are not insignificant background noise, nor distractions or childish ideas. They matter. They are messengers. They shouldn't be ignored but instead taken into your arms and then raised up higher, above the cold glare of other people's judgement, towards where the light and the warmth are, to where they can really grow and bloom.

Romanticising your life does not mean denying what is real and what is happening, of course. It does not mean obscuring the truth of this world, ignoring what is painful and cruel and unjust, insisting that everything is lovely and perfect all the time. It isn't avoidance or dishonesty. You don't romanticise to play pretend or regress into ignorance, but instead to soothe, to experiment, to live more lightly, doing better by others and making each day a little clearer and more real than it might have felt other-wise. You do this because you know that you don't want to live out the days of your life in self-punishment and small measures. Although your time here on this planet is not all that long, it can be plenty long enough if you go about the business of finding beauty, taking care of beauty and then creating more beauty for yourself and others. This can help you to feel brave and worthy, and to be a better force for patience and joy and peace in a world that so desperately needs more of these things.

Romanticising your life is not about daydreaming of better and then leaving it there, faint and one dimen-sional. The essence of romanticising your life is contained in the doing. It's not bookmarking the recipe and imag-ining some far-off evening when you sit down to eat it; it's buying the ingredients, turning on the radio and roll-ing up your sleeves to cook. It's not picturing yourself getting off the bus a few stops early and walking home from work through the park at golden hour; it's hitting the bell, thanking the driver and stepping down onto the pavement. It's not thinking about writing to the distant and missed relative, the best friend across the world, the partner travelling for work; it's buying the stamps and the stationary and putting pen to paper. It's doing all these things until they're practices, habits, things you can't remember a time when you didn't do.

In other words, you make it romantic by making it real.

It's also important to remember that making your life more romantic is not a temporary solution to being single or lonely, though it's a practice that can be especially helpful in those times. It isn't a stop gap until the real prize of love and popularity and happily ever after comes along. It's a way to live now and in the future – adding to the things that you already have, adorning your days and your surroundings and your relationships for the long haul.

Romanticising your life, therefore, begins with daily gestures. Hearing the start of a rainstorm, opening the window and leaning out to catch the drops. Ending a long and difficult day or week not by sinking into the sofa and scrolling your phone while reality TV plays in the background, but by filling the bath, lighting that expensive candle and soaking for two hours while reading a book. Buying yourself flowers – either the most decadent arrangement in the florist or the discounted bunch at the petrol station. Then, later, taking the nicest few from the bunch and pressing them into the pages of your heaviest book, keeping those dried petals somewhere safe as a reminder that although many beautiful things don't last very long, your memories of them can.

In essence, romanticising your life means figuring out what you really love – your favourite flowers, your favourite way to drink a martini, your favourite herbal tea, your favourite film, your favourite poem. It's having a signature scent, a party trick, a favourite well-worn joke, a well-practised karaoke song, an earnest compliment for every person you meet. It's also about trying out new things – flavours, cocktails, hobbies, music – until your familiarity with yourself grows and blooms. Romanticising your life can be playful, expansive, silly, significant. It can be about indulgence, personal reinvention, play, curiosity, style, self-love. It can be whatever you want or need it to be.

And so, this book is not a list of rules. It's not a test than can be passed or failed, a strict set of instructions that must be followed to the letter or else the whole thing will fall apart.

It's just a little nudge.

A suggestion of how, if you find yourself so inclined,

you might make your life just a touch more romantic.

Sometimes the practice of romanticising a life can be a way back home, back into your body, towards your most treasured and longstanding relationships, reuniting you with your goals and sense of purpose. Sometimes it can simply be a reason to get up out of bed and into the world on days when you'd much rather shut the curtains and go back to sleep. It can help you to see more of the city or town where you live, perhaps leading you to fascinating local characters you might otherwise never have met. It may be a balm for the bad news stories that seem to beam endlessly out of our phones and television screens, its own kind of protest against what often feels like a relentlessly cruel and painful world. It can be a statement of intent: if the world is hard then you will be soft within it; you will add as much goodness to the landscape and the moment as possible, no matter how futile that might seem to certain people.

So no, there are no rules here. The words and advice in this book are just a road map for anyone who feels the pull of a sweeter and more beautiful life – one in which no apologies are made for moments of indulgence or fun, or efforts to feel romantic and special and joyful. It is a guide for anyone who has struggled to feel deserving of blissful moments, adventure, delight, peace or pleasure.

In researching and creating this book about the practice of romanticising life, I've found myself drawn towards poetry and as I read, I realised that there's already so much writing on this very thing – taking the ordinary parts of life and noticing the miraculous that is contained within. One poem on this subject is called, rather aptly, 'Love'. It was written by Alex Dimitrov and the structure is simple, it is a list of the things that he loves. Some notable examples from this list are dessert for breakfast, the extra glass of wine, anyone who cannot say goodbye, kissing. Google it and read it now if you have a few moments to spare. The rest of this page can wait.

The poem 'Love', in my opinion, is a triumph of romanticism, a celebration of the extraordinary ordinary and the ways that we can all live more fully in this world. Dimitrov makes no attempt to hide from what is difficult

 about human life – that it ends, that people are complex, that relationships are hard, that it very often hurts, that there is great injustice – but still he loves, he notices, he celebrates. Though he lists more than a hundred things, it still doesn't feel like it scratches the surface. There is so much to love, it turns out. I think his is a poem that invites each of us to begin crafting our own lists, to dedicate time to stopping, noticing, paying attention to the world around us. What would be on your list? What is it that you love about this place, this life, this day?

I could name so many more poems on this subject – 'What the Living Do' by Marie Howe, 'The Continuous Life' by Mark Strand, 'Fall Song' by Joy Harjo, 'You Can't Have It All' by Barbara Ras and 'Summer in a Small Town' by Tony Hoagland, which ends with the line: 'Now. Steal pleasure.'

This is what we are doing when we're engaged in the work of romanticising. We are leaping without looking into the days of our lives. We're stealing pleasure, understanding our bodies, our minds, our hearts and our time on earth in new and more vital ways. Softer, sweeter and more courageous ways. We're politely disagreeing with the widely held belief that beauty and spontaneity are only for certain people living certain lives – the young, the wealthy, the lucky and the chosen. Instead, we choose ourselves again and again, saying yes, saying now, saying that this quiet beauty and this feeling of belonging is for us, too. We learn how to feel more open to experience and experimentation, entirely allowed to be wherever and whoever we are. It is obeying sensation instead of sense, giving to ourselves what we are tired of waiting for from others.

Living like this is what helped return me to the world when I most wanted to leave it and it is what keeps me here now, two feet on the ground, eyes open, seeing not only what is there but what else could be if only I keep going, keep trying, keep painting more vivid colours on top of the canvas of this life. It is not me trying to escape where I am but rather to make that place better, brighter, more beautiful. To some, it may look like radical change, a total upheaval of one way of living and a replacement with another. For others, it will be a tweaked mindset, something to ponder now and again. It will look different for each of us and is, I believe, made more beautiful in its variations.

So why not give it a try? Turn these pages and see what happens. Why not experiment with romanticising, making your days sweeter in whichever ways you're able to, treasuring the normal, miraculous parts of

your normal, miraculous life, holding on tight to the
souvenirs that say:

I was here, I lived, I did so on purpose.

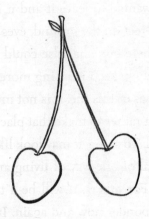

The Best Things in Life Are Free

Living intentionally and romantically can initially feel like a call towards consumption, just another excuse to tap into all the latest trends and satisfy the urge to acquire new belongings: clothes, art, furniture, cosmetics, trinkets, books, things. It's easy enough to justify this mindset, especially at the start of the process. You can tell yourself: These purchases are necessary. I need them to make my new, shiny, romantic life a reality. Just one more of this, another of that and then I'll be done. Then I'll have all that I need. Then I'll have arrived.

And sometimes this may well be the case. As more and more people are now renting and/or house sharing into their twenties and thirties, it is true that there are real emotional benefits to making our spaces feel more our own, more under our control, and filling them with carefully chosen things that indicate that we are home. Similarly, getting a costly new tattoo or expensive haircut can be a significant moment in you becoming yourself – a tangible embodiment of the transition that you're attempting to make from being a distant observer of your life to an active and present participant in it. Maybe buying certain makeup and experimenting with how you look will be a vital part of a more romanti-

24

cised life, allowing you to learn how to present yourself outwardly the way you've always felt inwardly. If you have spent years talking yourself out of it and living frugally, a romantic and courageous act could be finally allowing yourself to spend a bit of money on yourself and your interests.

Perhaps there is a practical element to this too. Such as getting some new gadgets for the kitchen so you can finally realise your dreams of spending Sunday mornings baking, for example. Or maybe a shiny bike is the entry point to a more expansive life, a way to get you out of the house and into the world, growing braver in your exploration and helping to heal your relationship with exercise. Maybe it's a record player and a stack of vinyl records you're dreaming of, forgoing the ease of music streaming services and engaging with albums in their entirety. Maybe it's a camera, an easel and a new set of paints, a three-month ceramics course, a bow and arrow, a chef's knife, a shovel, a pair of running shoes, a chessboard.

There's no shame in having these desires for new things or new experiences; no need to apologise for wanting to pick up a hobby or spend your own money on having fun and deepening your interests. This isn't greed or needless consumption; it's expansion, exploration. But there may also be other, more fleeting impulses, and these we need to learn to steer clear of.

Buying pile after pile of factory-fresh clothing, for example, can be a tempting but ultimately wasteful and misguided way of trying to romanticise your life. Following trends and creating endless new outfits may *seem* necessary in helping you to make your dream life into a reality, but poorly stitched garments quickly lose their appeal and turn into clutter, and are then shipped off to far-off landfill sites or charity shops where they languish in sad heaps of fast fashion. It can be difficult to resist, of course, especially with the number of ads we're fed each day for new clothes and accessories, new trends that we simply must keep up with.

You'll be bored and restless at home one night and the algorithm will seem to sense it, serving you up a link and a discount code at precisely your weakest and most dissatisfied moment. The blazer you've been coveting for weeks, that you can imagine yourself wearing as you sit in a cafe and journal on a rainy day, the big sunhat you could pose underneath on the beach, the crossbody bag for those European music festivals you might go to in a year or so. Or perhaps you'll be feeling a little weird about your body, tired of how your clothes feel, and just then an influencer will post an affiliate link for a summer dress that suddenly feels like the only thing you will ever want to wear – a dress that would be perfect for wading through long meadow grass as you search for a place to have a picnic, or attending a wedding, or riding a horse along a beach. It might be skincare or expensive treatments that call to you, a new fourteen-step skincare routine of shimmery potions and lotions that you let yourself believe will be the ones that finally transform you, ushering in a new era of self-care and self-preservation, an outer glow to coax out your inner one.

And again: there is no need to beat yourself up for having these desires. Most of us do! But it remains important that you try to be mindful of the power these desires have and the directions in which they can take you. By sitting with the feelings and allowing the most fleeting of them to pass, you can learn to make more considered choices about what you want your romanticising journey to look like. You can avoid making the same mistakes over and over again, wasting your money and then finding that you're still just as unfulfilled as before, that pile of shoddily made objects and fast fashion pieces representing nothing but out-of-control consumerism, which is about as far from romantic living as you can get.

As we move through this process of trying to live more romantically and mindfully, the distinctions between worthy purchases and needless waste get easier to make. Buying something you've long wanted or putting money behind a new hobby or practice can absolutely be what it takes to bring you closer to a fuller and more romantic life, connected to your passions. Sometimes, though, it's just an expensive and ethically questionable distraction from the real work of making your life more romantic by slowly and deliberately discovering a better way of being in and seeing the world.

My own expensive missteps and impulse buys have taught me that a truly beautiful romantic philosophy is often centred around what is already here, what is already owned and in reach, what can be carefully considered, treasured and kept for the long term. Like any mindfulness practice, this is a process of gradually increasing your awareness and patience, as a means of living more peacefully, easily and happily. It's opening your eyes to the beauty, peace and joy that you already have free and immediate access to – the local lido or swimming pond, the sunset, the sunrise, the kindness of strangers, the pen and paper, the paintbrush and the canvas, the trees, the birds singing, the smile exchanged with a stranger, the reunion with a loved one, the favourite old song coming on the radio just a moment after you heard it playing in your mind. It can be as simple as opening a window, as bold as joining a picket line, as traditional as handwriting a letter to an older relative who you know will feel genuinely touched by the gesture. It may also involve focusing on your own pleasure and care – giving yourself a manicure or a pedicure, smearing on a fruity face mask from the back of the drawer, getting into the bath and taking your time to scrub and buff and soak, treating your body like a loved and precious thing.

At work, a place most of us spend a great deal of our waking hours, accessing even glimmers of romance might require being more assertive with your boss or your colleagues about the time that belongs solely to you, time that should not be interrupted by the non-urgent machinations of your workplace. It could look like asking for the promotion you know you want or requesting more accommodations and support so that you're less anxious and harried. It could mean a kind word, a sweet gesture to a colleague who you know is having a hard day. It may even mean taking the steps necessary to leave.

In your daily life, perhaps you can simply relax your criteria for what constitutes a really good day, pulling your gaze away from what can't be controlled (the weather, other people's actions, the availability of your favourite fizzy drink in the corner shop) and focus on what is real and true and here. Ask: How can I connect more fully to this moment? What beauty might I be overlooking? How can I make this day or place or situation better for others alongside myself? What am I yet to see?

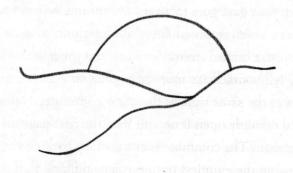

LITTLE WINS

A day that might feel familiar: you wake up and immediately reach for the phone that's under your pillow, seeing blue light before you see daylight, your eyes instantly full of bad news from every major news organisation. You check the apps. Red hearts on one of your photos, three new spam emails – free air fryer! Final demand! One weird trick to banish cellulite right down into Hell forever! – a reminder of a dentist appointment, a confirmation of a second date you don't really want to go on, a friend's birthday last week that you totally forgot to send a card or message for.

On the packed train to work, your chin drops to your chest, your gaze goes to where your phone is in your lap. There's a well-reviewed book at the bottom of your bag that you've carried around for weeks but you leave it where it is, tell yourself it's more important to read the headlines at the same time as the other commuters, but that you'll definitely open it up and read the first page on the way home. The commute is automatic – parking the car, choosing the emptiest train carriage, walking to the bus stop, tapping your foot impatiently because the queue at the cafe is moving at a snail's pace. You get to work without focusing on a single face, without looking around, without smiling, without thinking about anything much at all. There might have been a musician at the train station with an open guitar case, a warm smile, but your headphones were in and the crowd was surging all around you and there wasn't time, because there's never time.

There is no shame or blame if this is familiar to you. So many of us live some days on autopilot, just getting by and keeping the cogs turning. Sometimes there's nothing else for it. We're so often not free to do as we please whenever we please – we must work to support ourselves and our families, to remain housed and fed and stable. We're not bound only to our romantic whims but to the demands of bosses, the call of deadlines, debts, dependents. But there are ways, both small and great, to keep a hold of greater shares of joy and romance, love and vitality.

You can emancipate yourself a little from the clutches of social media overstimulation and compulsion by leaving your phone at home or swapping your sim card into some older tech so you're less likely to be swallowed into an Instagram hole instead of seeing and taking part in the world around you. You can try going to sleep or waking up an hour earlier, or incorporating a much-needed summer siesta or a walk in the park into your usual routine at least one afternoon each week. You can do more reading, more movie watching, more sightseeing, more quick phone catchups with friends, more homemade juices, more meditation. You can also rest more, giving to your body the moments of peace and slowing down that it has probably been asking you for.

Romance can be in the disruption of your usual routines, in the small tweaks you make here and there that help you to break out of a rut or open up your life just that tiny bit more. Romanticising the more ordinary moments of life doesn't mean you have to make your existence here any smaller. It doesn't mean you need to give up any of your ambitions, your career dreams or grand future plans. You can still seek out epic loves and wondrous trips to far-off lands, deepening self-knowledge and growth at the same time as you try to romanticise the little things and teach yourself to notice the romance in the everyday more closely. You can grow your gratitude for the ordinary without dialling back your hunger, your drive or your imagination. Beginning with the little things can be a great way to crack open the world and see how much more there is to have, to enjoy, to keep, to love. This will draw you closer to the immediate beauty of the place and time that you find yourself in, encouraging you to be grateful for it and to use it as a starting point for even greater adventures.

If you look, you'll find that these little wins are everywhere, and they all begin with noticing, with slowing things down, with seeing what can be done with what's already here. It can happen while you hang out a load of clean washing in the garden or by the window on a warm day and feel grateful for your hands and your fingers, grateful for the fresh, nostalgic smell of the fabric softener, grateful for the air, for the sky, for the sun and the warmth that will dry the denim, the linen, the cotton, the lucky underwear that is falling apart at the seams but that you're not quite yet ready to part with. You can be grateful for the clothes that are yours to wear as you wish, clothes that perhaps once belonged to someone else but now belong to you, are now in your care, clothes you can mix and match to create your outfits, which you will wear out there in the world – moving, living, being with the people you love.

Romance can be in the routines – in the slow and deliberate preparing of a delicious breakfast every Sunday morning while the radio plays, for example. Decorating a stack of thick, fluffy pancakes with edible flowers and a chopped banana formed into a smiley face, then topping the whole thing off with an aesthetically pleasing drizzle of maple syrup. Taking a picture for your sixty-nine Instagram followers and for your grandma, who likes to know you're looking after yourself, eating the most important meal of the day.

It makes life so much richer when you do this, when you train your eyes towards the little but lovely things, guiding your love and attention to subtler pleasures and less showy victories. It does a heart and a body good to live like this, adding so much more to the tally of good things, stacking the odds towards gratitude and happiness in a way that only chasing grand, enormous goals can't.

Here are some places to start if you want to begin romanticising your life for free(ish):

Nature

Getting out into nature is one of the best no-cost ways to begin living a more romantic life.

One of my favourite ways to get some fresh air is to take myself on a 'romance walk'. A romance walk is a slight twist on a concept called 'the weird walk' that I've borrowed from a friend. To take a weird walk, you leave the house, go for a wander around and try to spot as many strange, fascinating or funny things as possible. An old doll's head that a bird has a made a nest out of? Check.

A graffitied love note on a wall from Gavin apologising for what happened in Margate in 2007 and imploring Hannah to give him another chance? Check. Miniature dancing electronic Christmas trees available for purchase during a July heatwave? Check. You get the drift. In my more romantic version of this (already excellent) idea, I go out on a walk and I look for the lovely things, the things that remind me that the world is full of beauty and goodness and wonder. Two people kissing on a corner, for example, someone sharing their umbrella with a stranger, two birds leaning against one another on the bough of a blossoming tree or a child tilting their ice cream towards a younger sibling so they can have the first taste. You can even incorporate it into otherwise dreary walks or trips outside of the house – the trudge to the post office or the fifteen-minute stretch between the bus stop and work.

Another free way to enjoy yourself in nature is by searching online for nearby public trails or historic walks through your city or town. Either grab a friend or go alone, taking a snack, a coffee (or a hip flask of whiskey) and a playlist of your favourite songs. Immerse yourself in the walk, intentionally looking out for things that you'd otherwise miss – and perhaps have been missing for years – and learning more about the place where you've built this part of your life, its history and links to other places. You can go even further with this – what poems or plays have been written about your city? Which films have been set or filmed there? Is there anyone famous who was born there? Go and hunt out lesser-known places to sit or read or walk, that you can then refer to as 'your spots' and show to people when they come to visit.

You can also see if there are local volunteer services you can join, perhaps helping to clean up a local area, or donating your time to wildlife preservation or urban ecology. Not only is this a lovely way to do more during a time when we all need to pitch in, it can also be great for both your physical and your emotional health, slowing you down and connecting you to the most fundamental realities of the world and your place in it.

Technology

Though modern technology *can* often and easily be a source of deep misery and cruel comparison, it also has some fairly miraculous applications. When else in human history have you been able to sit on the sofa, the train or the toilet and with just a few taps of your fingers, tell half a dozen people in your life just how much you love and cherish them? And yet so often we don't use it like this. Instead, we browse for things we don't need or read about what banal thing one banal rich celebrity said about another banal rich celebrity, or argue with a stranger about the correct way to pronounce a word that didn't even exist until a few years ago. Instead of reaching out we turn inwards, instead of connecting we distance.

But that can change! It can change right now! You don't have to become a total compliment pest but, now and again, why not make the effort to send a handful of loving, generous, thoughtful texts out into the ether? Or maybe there's an elderly relative you can call to ask about their day? Perhaps you could leave an entertaining voice note for someone who you know is feeling down, or simply vocalise to the people you love that they matter to you, reminding them of a funny moment you shared, telling them earnestly that you're excited for the next time your paths cross, imparting a bit of wisdom or sharing a fact that you know will excite and delight them.

Another way to use technology to romanticise your life is to simply . . . not use it at all. By turning off your phone now and again – not just putting it on airplane mode or hiding it at the bottom of your bag but shutting it off entirely and placing it out of sight – you can invite so much more of the immediate world into your eyeline. This doesn't have to mean a total upheaval of your digital life or an eschewing of technology to the point where you can't even remember what a meme is. You can just tweak your screen time a little and see if it helps, see if you're better able to feel present. Start by leaving your phone at home for the day or the afternoon, or just turning it off at set times of the day – perhaps for your commute to or from work or the first and last two waking hours of each day over the weekend.

You can set firmer boundaries around having it on at dinner parties, weddings and other social events, too, instead focusing on conversation and in-person connection. You can commit to separating yourself from your screens when you're spending time with older relatives or people you don't get to see very often, enjoying genuine quality time with them instead of giving in to the urge to drift off into your various apps. Nix the temptation for a quick scroll by switching off and then sitting with whatever discomfort that arises. Because a romantically realised life is a life of noticing and being present, and though it can be lovely to document the big moments with photos or videos, staring for hours down at a screen can mean we miss key moments and so many of the subtle joys of life.

You can also try to bring other people in on it, having intentionally phone-free evenings or days with your friends, partner or family. Consider switching to film or digital cameras if you want a record of your time together. You can throw dinner parties where all your phones go into a bowl on top of the cupboard (covered with cling film or foil if you know you or someone else might have particularly itchy fingers after a few hours). Grab a mate and go for a morning walk to a coffee shop, leaving your devices behind at home and rewarding yourself with a delicious brunch, with no way to give in to phone-based temptations.

Utilising slightly older technology can also be a great way to access an extra bit of romance without going totally pre-digital. Use an iPod or another almost-defunct-but-not-quite-yet MP3 player to soundtrack your walks. You can source a CD or record player for your parties or evenings at home, both helping to keep you in the moment and also adding a bit of nostalgic wonder to the event, inviting you to go through old boxes of discs at charity shops or in the attic, then actually choosing what you'll listen to rather than relying on an algorithm.

Music

Although music streaming subscriptions aren't technically free, I think we can give this one a pass since most of us have them or share them with others. Soundtracking your life is an easy and effective way to tap into the beauty of it, to elevate or deepen a feeling or a moment or a journey, and something that can be really joyful and educational in the planning. Make playlists for anything and everything – both the big moments and the small. Make playlists for walks you'll take, in the sun and the rain, through piles of dropped autumn leaves or along distant shores. Make a playlist for your commute to and from work, your journey to and from first dates, themed dinner parties you haven't yet thrown but want to, romantic encounters that may not currently be on your radar but that you trust are coming. Make playlists full of all the songs that you can remember loving as a child – what used to play on the car radio or from your parents' tape

or CD player during those magical years when you were growing up and first figuring out what it was you liked and didn't like. Make playlists of the songs or albums that your grandparents played in the house or in the car, all the songs that you made up elaborate dance routines to in your bedroom with your best friend after school.

Create playlists for and with other people too – your best friend or your sister/brother or your girlfriend/ boyfriend or anyone who you love. Take it in turns to add songs until you've made something that perfectly fits your shared mood and tastes. Introduce one another to your favourite and most treasured songs – the songs

43

you listen to when you're sad, when you're happy, when you need a boost, when you want to think of a particular time in your life, when you're looking for inspiration. You can even make an evening out of it: turning the lights down and lying down together in a nest of cushions and blankets, just listening – no skipping, no complaining, no other distractions (besides perhaps a nice bottle of wine and some snacks).

You can also discover new favourites, searching the internet for 'best albums of all time' or 'best lesser-known albums of the last decade' or 'greatest songs since the end of the Palaeolithic era' or some variation of that, and making a checklist you can work your way through at your own pace. See how many you can listen to over a weekend or try to listen to just one a week for the rest of the year.

Also, keep an eye out for nearby venues – pubs or bars or parks – that have regular and free live music. Go with your mates, have a ball and discover some new songs and artists without spending the earth on gig tickets (though it's always good form to tip or offer the musicians a pint once they've finished playing).

Culture

Search for what's happening now and what's coming up in your local area or the city or town where you live: art shows, history exhibits, free talks, music festivals, fairs. Mark the most intriguing ones on your calendar now so that you don't have to go hunting for them later and can act on a spontaneous urge to get out and do something cultural, see something beautiful or have your mind or heart opened.

Go to a gallery and try not to behave like a bored kid on a school trip. Channel the energy of a time-traveller or an alien seeing human art for the first time. Move from room to room, carefully choosing your favourite works of art or the historical artefacts you find most meaningful. Find the painting that moves you the most, sit down in front of it and really look at it. Read the little plaque that tells you about it, take a picture of it on your phone, think about it on the way home, take your friends to see it and be thankful that someone decided that instead of not painting it that they would paint it instead. Find beautiful things and build ongoing relationships with them.

Other people

One of the best entirely free ways to make your life better and more joyful is to smile at the people you pass as you go about your day. Don't worry if they don't smile in return – that's not the point of this exercise. Just smile and let that be the whole and completed gesture. Smile and know that yes, though it could have been met with indifference or scorn the minute they passed out of sight, it could also have been received with delight, gifting the recipient a slightly renewed sense of hope in the general goodness of people. So, smile and smile and smile some more.

You can also invite extra romance into your life by writing down your number on a piece of paper or card and keeping it safely tucked in your purse or wallet, just in case you ever want to give it to a good-looking stranger. Whether you're shy or anxious or just dislike the idea of bothering someone out in public, this is a memorable and respectful way to shoot your shot with them. All it takes is a deep breath, a smile and for you to hand it over. You can do this on the move too, as you're getting off the train or the bus, or leaving the cafe that you've both been sitting in. And whether they text or call you is beside the point: it's the doing that matters; this is what opens you up to more joy, more excitement and more romance.

Another free exercise is writing yourself a sort of bingo card at the start of each year of things you hope to experience or see out in the world. Things like a couple's first kiss, your own first kiss with a new person, someone smiling goofily at their phone so distracted they almost walk into a lamp-post, two strangers dressed incredibly similarly standing next to one another in public, someone paying for a stranger's order at a cafe. Someone riding a unicycle, a reunion at a train station or airport, a stranger complimenting another stranger on their outfit, someone trying a new food for the first time and loving it,

someone trying a new food for the first time and hating it. The perfect pink and purple evening sky, a tree wearing green, yellow, orange and red leaves all at once. Groups of friends laughing so hard together that they can't speak coherently, a baby's toothy grin or laugh, an older couple holding hands as they walk together, someone crying in the cinema. A sunset, a sunrise, a couple on a date comparing the sizes of their hands, a dog in a raincoat, children waving at you from the windows of buses or trains, your own hands waving back.

SOME MORE SMALL, FREE PLEASURES

The smell of clean bedclothes after they've been dried out in the sun

I don't know what it is that makes sun-dried laundry smell that much better than laundry dried inside or in a machine, but it's an inarguable fact that it does. Perhaps it's living in a country where so often the sun doesn't shine that makes it an even more precious sensation. All I know is that when I'm bringing my air-dried sheets inside, I almost immediately assume the role of one of those actors in an advert, burying my full face into the fabric, inhaling as though I'm a strait-jacketed magician who's just smashed their way out of a fish tank after being submerged for a worrying period of time, sighing with a pantomime satisfaction that I couldn't hide even if I wanted to.

Getting a text out of the blue from the person you were just thinking about

Whether you're the kind of person who chalks this up to a spiritual or psychic tether between yourself and the people you love or if you'd just call it coincidence, there's something so lovely and reassuring about knowing that you've occurred to someone else at almost exactly the same moment as they've occurred to you. It's a reminder that we are, in fact, on our loved ones' minds and in their thoughts, even when we're not right in front of them, and that there are people in the world that care enough about us to reach out, even if they don't have anything to say beyond 'hello' or 'I miss you' or 'just saw a funny looking dog on the bus that looked exactly like you lol xxx'.

Witnessing something funny and sharing a wordless smile about it with a stranger

Getting the giggles in public is already one of life's greatest little joys, but doing so with someone you've never met can be even lovelier. It's a moment that reminds us that strangers aren't background actors or lesser characters in the world – they're human beings just like us, with their own senses of humour and ability to see the daily silliness of life on earth. It's a fleeting connection – soon enough, the funny moment passes and you're both back in your own minds and on your own journeys, but it's so lovely while it's happening.

Finding something once treasured that you thought was lost forever, perhaps had even forgotten about

This usually happens during a spring clean or a move: trinkets rediscovered at the back of drawers or under beds, scribbled Post-it note reminders, misplaced jewellery, novelty hats from trips you took with friends, party favours, wedding invites, phone numbers, photos, fridge magnets, love letters, postcards. It's a way to travel back through time, each item like a gift from some past version of you.

A great first kiss
This is especially magical if it's a kiss that feels like it's been building all evening, or perhaps even longer than that, a sort of magnetic thread that runs between your lips and someone else's lips, a charge that only you and they know anything about. A great first kiss doesn't have to be technically flawless to be perfect – it just needs to involve that energy, that excitement.

Homemade cards and drawings from children
If you're a parent this one might be a little less of a joy, but for relatives or those without children, there can be something so precious about receiving a scribbly, smeary drawing of what looks like an onion ring wearing a wedding dress on a crumpled, damp, half-chewed up piece of paper, and having a child look up at you with deep sincerity in their eyes and hearing them say, 'Here, I drew this picture of you.'

Being outside when the leaves start dropping in the autumn
For a lot of us, the transition from warmer seasons into colder seasons can take an emotional toll, and so finding

little, beautiful things to cling on to can make the difference between having a good day and a really bad one. Having yellow and orange whipped around me by a cool, autumn breeze is one such little thing.

When a typically standoffish and bad-tempered cat takes a particular liking to you

When this happens, you feel like the chosen one, the master of all humankind, the sole tamer of the hissing beast. Whether it's because you were, in fact, an Egyp-

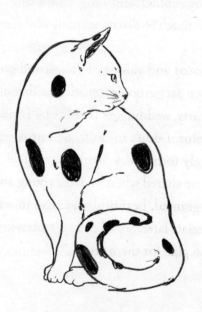

tian emperor in a previous life or because you still smell vaguely like tuna from the sandwich you made earlier doesn't matter. It only matters that you were chosen and nobody can take that away from you.

Hitting repeat for the very first time on a song that you know is going to be one of your favourites

The best thing about this one is that it is guaranteed to happen again and again in your life. Even if the song becomes unlistenable through overuse it's okay. Because there will be another, and another, and another after that. There is so much to discover and love.

Taking photos and videos of your loved ones

It's a known fact among my friends that at any event – birthday party, wedding, trip to Ikea – I will pester them all for photos. I don't mean to be intrusive; I just know we are likely to one day want a record of the ordinary moments we shared when we were young and taking that youth for granted, beautiful and alive in ways we might only appreciate later. So, take the pictures, keep them safe. You'll be so glad for them later.

Taking a photo of somebody you really love, helping them see themselves the way you see them

With high quality camera phones permanently attached to our hands it can often feel mundane and even annoying to have your picture taken. It's nothing to take a picture, the work of a couple of seconds, and it's so easy to then forget it. But sometimes it can be more than that, capturing a person in a moment of pure bliss, just as radiant and beautiful in the photo as you see them in person.

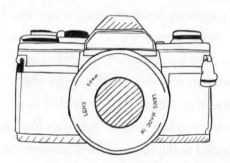

Sharing inside jokes with your friends that are so old and worn that nobody can remember where they came from and are impossible to explain but still make you cry-laugh

Sometimes, the smallest reference to an old joke or comedic bit can set a whole group going – a phrase or song lyric, a gesture or even just the particular intonation of a vowel sound. Jokes like this can age as you age, wearing in like a thick knitted jumper. They are ways to time-travel without moving, tethering you tighter to your friends and your shared history with them.

Journalling

Keeping a diary isn't for everyone. Growing up, I could never quite make it stick. I'd certainly try, would faithfully document my days for a week or two at a time, writing down what I ate, all my various emotions and observations, if I saw the person I fancied, if I had decided that I wanted to grow up and be a juggler or a hedgehog. But then I would miss a day, and then another, and then another after that. After enough blank spaces, it would feel like it was too late to pick the diary back up and it would be added to the pile of 'failed' attempts.

What I've learned from my many attempts to journal like a pro is that it really helps if you don't treat journalling as a chore or a daily obligation, but rather as an invitation to slow down as needed, to pick up a pen, set it to paper and just see what happens. Done right, journalling can be a truly leisurely activity, an opportunity to step out of this world and into another, to get curious about your-self, to seek pleasure in writing about your life, working through your feelings, memories and experiences. If it doesn't come naturally to you to journal every day, then so be it – release that expectation and try something else. Perhaps try assigning yourself a weekly timeslot, planned around your existing routine.

Perhaps you'd like to park yourself and your notebook in front of some reality TV and write freely, or pour a glass of wine, light a candle and sit down at the table with a blank page and your favourite pen. Or maybe you need to allow yourself to pick it up and put it down with total freedom, sometimes writing every single day for a month but other times leaving your journal unopened for weeks and weeks at a time. Alternatively, you could try packing it in every bag and just seeing if the mood takes you when you're out in the world.

You can use prompts or just free-write, putting pen to paper and seeing what happens. Some of your entries may be detailed, pages and pages long, using your best pen and your neatest handwriting, with every tiny detail of your day accounted for. Others may just be scribbled notes, almost unreadable, recording moments you want to remember, passing irritations, meals you had, jokes you've heard that you want to later pass off as your own.

You might prefer to write your journal on your phone or laptop, using an app or just by emailing yourself or opening a Word document. Or you could buy a sketchpad and make it into a kind of scrapbook, sticking or clipping in receipts from first dates or birthday meals, ticket stubs, photobooth snaps, sticky-note love letters, your grandma's handwriting torn from the bottom corner of an old birthday card – an 'I love you' that you know remains true even if she's no longer here to say it. A journal can be a place to plant these little but significant mementoes so that they have a chance to grow into solid memories, keeping them from being lost in the shuffle of time.

Journalling on the move is a great way to maintain it as a regular habit. If ever I'm on a long train journey I try to dedicate at least an hour to scribbling away in my journal. This can take a bit of willpower initially, but once you've built it into a habit then it's far easier to return to. And yes, you will have to find a way to ignore the fact that your phone is right there in your pocket or bag or on the little tray table. To start with, it will probably feel far more tempting to scroll mindlessly on these journeys –

looking at the cheery holiday snaps or wedding pictures of acquaintances or old colleagues, or reading celebrity headlines, or swiping this way and that way on a dating app. Make a compromise with yourself – perhaps you'll journal for thirty minutes, then do something else. Or you'll only look at your phone for the first or last hour of your journey. Because journalling on a train is the ideal time to get some of your thoughts down on paper. You've got nowhere else to be and a whole world passing by out of the window if you need the inspiration. You can take the time to write poems or memories or erotic fan fiction or even just spill your current feelings onto a page – nobody but you will know. Make it an indulgence too; buy yourself a coffee and a pile of snacks, press play on a favourite album and see what happens when you put pen to paper.

There will be journal prompts throughout this book, which you are free to use or ignore. These are prompts that I've used myself and continue to use, little nudges to get my brain and writing hand going. I write whenever I feel like it, and this is a system that works for me. I also try not to feel self-conscious about what ends up on the page – either because it's very little or because it feels like far too much. I remind myself that I'm not writing to impress anyone or prove anything about myself or my character. I'm writing simply because it helps me to hold on tighter to details and to better focus my energy and my attention towards the things that matter, the things that might otherwise be overshadowed or edged out by the petty stresses of life.

When choosing a journal to dedicate to romanticising your life, I'd recommend something small and tough, something that can be slipped into pockets and packs, that can endure a bit of battering, some spilt drinks or a spot of bad weather.

Here are some journal prompts to help you to romanticise your day-to-day life and to create more romance for the future:

List five things that you feel grateful for in this moment.

....

....

....

....

....

Describe what your ideal spring day looks like.

....

....

....

....

List ten new things you'd like to try this year.

....

....

....

....

....

....

....

....

....

....

Instead of scrolling on your phone when you next have
a bit of time to yourself, what would you like to try?

....

....

....

What are your favourite things about this time of year?

....

....

The best things in life are free and to you those
things are . . .

....

....

....

....

What aspect of your life are you most grateful
for right now?

....

....

....

....

List your favourite places to go and be with your thoughts.

....

....

....

How can you make more time for yourself and your peace of mind each week?

....

....

....

....

What are you currently looking forward to?

....

....

....

....

Modern Dating (Minus the Misery)

The world can open wide when we travel and explore, and it can also open wide when we fall in love and find someone (or multiple someones) to see it with. Love and relationships are perhaps the most obvious and immediate associations you might have with 'romance', yet it can feel nearly impossible to square that word with the way that dating looks and feels in our modern age. These days, dating so often begins and ends with pixels or words on a screen, plans spoken of but never quite followed through on, dating app matches made and then lost, remade and then lost once more, the progression of each relationship mapped in messages sent and received. Hey, how's your day going? becoming Do you fancy grabbing a drink this week? becoming That was fun. We should do it again sometime becoming Can I see you this weekend? becoming I know it's late but do you want to come over . . . ? becoming Sorry just seeing this now – I've been so busy at work becoming Yeah – maybe. Can I let you know nearer the time? becoming 'message seen' becoming . . . nothing at all, a space where a person briefly was and then is not, just another ghost. Under these conditions, it's easy to understand why, despite the apparent abundance of possible ways to meet and connect, so many people are experiencing feelings of isolation, believing that there isn't much romance left in the search for love.

It's true that dating in the 2020s can often feel bleak and drained of magic, a carousel of disappointment and dashed hope that we're all doomed to go on riding indefinitely. It seems like love is no longer about chance, fate, eye contact held across a smoky and crowded dance hall. Now it's about staying on the algorithm's good side, periodically updating and tweaking your profile, wearily doing your hair for your sixth first date of the month. It's not soul connections, it's WIFI connections. It's not happily ever after, it's happy hour after happy hour, sharing cheap drinks with a different (mis)match every other Thursday. It's an ever-growing list of snappy (and often depressing) terms to memorise and fear – ghosting, snow storming, love bombing, gaslighting, future faking, oystering, icing, groundhogging, catfishing, half-masting, breadcrumbing, cobwebbing, guardrailing, negging – definitions merging and mixing, often transforming a fun new crush into a list of potential misdeeds and transgressions – things to be wary of before you've even hugged hello and sat down beside them at the pub or bar.

My own dating history has been a patchwork of good and bad, amazing and terrible – uninspiring situation-ships, near misses, some disastrous dates – but many great ones too – sweet but fleeting encounters, serious relationships, deep and buoyant loves followed by gutting and terrible heartbreaks. I've had my fair share of romantic pain and my fair share of romantic joy. There have been some moments when I've felt in control, wise and so close to the fairytale that I could taste it. And there have been other moments when I've genuinely despaired, wondering if there was something I was missing or getting wrong, if that was why love and dating so rarely felt the way I'd imagined it would.

Growing up in the 1990s meant that my idea of romantic love was shaped for me in writers' rooms, animation studios and on film sets. As a little girl, I watched VHS tapes of cartoon princesses on the crackly television set in the living room. I saw them languishing in castles and in cellars, saw how they only really came alive when their prince would appear in the forest or at the foot of the stairs to claim and complete them. I saw that a human life could be separated into two parts – before love and then after it. Before love was often a lightless place, a held breath, a halfway state. To be in the before of love would mean walking through the world alone, existing as part of a thing that was always designed to be bigger. It was time that could only become worthwhile retroactively, acquiring meaning only once you had met someone and fallen in love. When this happened, the second act would begin – which was the better and more real of the two. The *happily* and the *ever* and the *after*. That was what I wanted. That was what I had to start looking for.

Films continued to act as my compass as I progressed through my teenage years. The animated wildlife and yellow-haired cartoon damsels became brooding actors and weeping actresses. I watched eleventh-hour dashes through airports, rain-drenched kisses, shouted objections during marriage vows, fake orgasms in sandwich shops and impassioned speeches about seeing all of someone's flaws and loving them anyway. I saw these films and began to build my beliefs about love around their scenes. I'd sometimes skip an afternoon of school just to lie on the sofa or in bed and watch romcoms – The Notebook, When Harry Met Sally, Notting Hill, 10 Things I Hate About You. I wasn't that particular about a film's cast or the dialogue or soundtrack, but one thing I did absolutely insist on was a happy ending.

My need for romantic fulfilment and true love's enduring power was so great that on every viewing of Titanic I would turn off the television and eject the disk right after Jack and Rose have steamy sex in the stowed Coupé de Ville. In this way, I could overrule both James Cameron's direction and the facts of history itself, and choose my own ending, one in which there was no iceberg, no catastrophe, no floating door, no (spoiler alert) traumatic death scene in the cold and unforgiving water of the North Atlantic. I could imagine Rose dumping her shithead fiancé and sailing with Jack for the remaining five days. I could imagine them eating together at the buffet, dancing up a storm below deck, spitting and dolphin spotting in total bliss before arriving in New York together. There they would get married, make beautiful redheaded babies and live a long and loving life together, perhaps taking a cruise every April to mark their anniversary until they died in each other's arms at the ripe old age of 145. In the twenty-plus years since *Titanic* was released, despite sitting down to watch it many times, I've seen that final hour perhaps only three or four times. Happy ever after is a hard habit to break.

As a young person, films and television offered me the fix of romance that wasn't yet available to me in reality. For most of my adolescence, I found boys my age frustrating and careless; though, thankfully I felt protected from a lot of their cruelty by an unshakeable belief that I would have a dizzying future romance, that there was no other way my life could unfold. I participated in early adolescent dating on the off-chance that I was destined for a childhood-sweethearts-turned-love-story-for-the-ages plot, but I didn't worry when it never quite mate-rialised, when, aged fourteen, I wasn't rushing home like my friends to talk to a particular boy on the computer or chang-

ing my screen name to say: »—(¯`v´¯)—» taken x Darren's forever »—(¯`v´¯)—». I felt sure that if not now, then definitely later. I was a believer, a worshipper at the altar of true love, certain that romance would appear right on cue, arriving just in time, like the white limo at the end of *Pretty Woman*.

But as life went on and I spent more time worrying and waiting for a text back than I did blissfully in love and coupled up, my belief in love – the one that I'd orbited around for my entire childhood and so much of my early adulthood – began to wane, becoming faint and flickering where it had once been solid and inarguable. There were so many false starts, so much uncertainty that masqueraded as excitement, cruelty that masqueraded as passion. My hopes went up and came down, a nauseating fairground ride that I kept vowing to stay off but then found myself right back in line for.

Changing the whole culture of dating in the digital age may be a little ambitious but I believe that each of us can take steps to make the process less personally depressing and disheartening, restoring the romance to it gradually until it's something so deeply planted it can't be uprooted or ruined by something so mundane as a failed connection or a near-stranger's decision to behave cruelly or cowardly towards us.

So, yes, I know the situation can seem bleak and there's a lot to rightfully complain about in the world of dating. It can be cathartic to speak your truth and I encourage healthy complaining – vent away, share your experiences with your friends and don't be ashamed. People are often cruel and unpredictable, and that hurts!

BUT this doesn't mean that this is the only way it's destined to go, or that there's nothing you can do to make the process more enjoyable. I believe there's plenty to be done to help us actively resist the drudgery of dating in the 2020s – the impersonal, copy-and-paste conversations, the feelings of disposability and widespread cynicism, the brutal repetitiveness of it all. I believe we can start by romanticising it, finding ways to lean towards the lovely moments of connection and attraction, and firmly reject cycles of indifference and game-playing.

To romanticise romance, dating and the search for love isn't to retreat into fantasy or denial. It doesn't require that you ignore what is hard or act like it doesn't sometimes totally suck. It's simply a way to build an armour against the petty rejections, the uninspiring cruelty, the rebuffs that sting but don't have to scar. It's also a way of putting a middle finger up to the idea that searching for love is a doomed endeavour. It's telling self-doubt, passivity and waiting to be chosen to fuck off and leave you to it. It's you deciding to be more assertive in dating, to only go where you're really wanted, taking the lead if necessary, rejecting what isn't meant for you and making your life romantic *now*, instead of waiting for someone else to do it.

My own journey to romanticise dating has taught me a lot about myself. I've learned that I don't want to wait for someone else to come along to help me start to heal and change, to feel myself chosen and worthy of love only when another person confirms it. I've learned that it is possible to begin that work at once, as a single person who wants love and believes deeply in it. In romanticising my pursuit of love, I've learned so much about what I want from a partner, what I need and what I will no longer accept or tolerate. I've daydreamed and soul-searched, I've set my intentions and I've worked very hard to heal my attachment wounds, and in doing this have given myself the opportunity to meet someone within that shifted perspective, within the space that I've made for myself. I've chosen to stop dating by numbers, to stop thinking of dating as means to an end – a stressful chore that I only put up with because I want to win the real prize of lifelong love and unbreakable romantic security.

Nowadays, I date because I enjoy it. I like to meet new people and I have a genuine curiosity about them. My belief in enduring love and partnership no longer feels faded and laced with cynicism. I know that good love exists, even when it's not in my immediate sights. And so I'm able to date without placing too much pressure on it, knowing that I just need to show up and see what could happen, rather than dating because I want to control the outcome. When I sit across a table and talk to a date, it's because I'm interested in finding out who they are, where they've been, what they think and believe. It's no longer a tense audition for either of us. I'm not there to prove my lovability and worth, and neither are they. Instead, we can meet each other at the intersection of curiosity and attraction, potential and possibility, catch and release. Maybe it'll be a mismatch, an awkward few hours that ends with a weird hug and a comedic retelling in your group chat. Or maybe it will be something else, something big and beautiful and loving that will open your world and heart wider than ever seemed possible. Maybe it will be something short lived yet lovely, a lesson contained in a casual but kind romance. You won't know what's waiting for you until you get out there and try.

You can't predict what's coming and you can't control what other people do. You can only focus on making yourself proud and doing yourself justice with your own actions and approach, by leading with love and with openness, by not accepting the unacceptable and letting go of what is so clearly not meant for you. You can make dating more romantic by taking it slowly, trying new things and learning the lessons that land on your doorstep and ask to come in. You can persist when it's difficult but also rest and withdraw when necessary.

You can also make dating and love more romantic by being clear about your desires from the outset, and refusing to abandon your values, self-esteem or emotional safety out of a desire to be chosen or validated. You can allow dating and meeting people to be more than just a frantic rush towards marriage or monogamy, and instead, a practice of exploring your desires, experimenting with your sexuality, firming up your boundaries, working on your communication skills and having your own back no matter what. Dating like this is something you can take care over and pride in, and it can help make so many other parts of your life more expansive and exciting. It can be a way to heal self-neglect, while moving beyond unworthy treatment and away from cycles of poor communication and doomed situationships.

Romantic love is not the only love worth nurturing, but it's more than okay if you crave it deeply and want to make the process easier to bear and more enjoyable. Here is everything I've learned about romanticising modern dating:

Romance belongs to you

Though most relationships tend to involve at least two people, it's important to remember that the romance you bring to a situation can be yours and yours alone. If someone chooses to behave unkindly or in confusing ways, they don't get to retain ownership of all of the loveliness that you brought and that you tried to create for the both of you.

Last year, I was on a work trip when I got talking to a man in a bar. It was the kind of romcom set up I'd daydreamed about ever since I'd gotten my flight confirmation: my eyes meeting their eyes across a busy bar, shy smiles exchanged, a moment where both of us wondered what would happen, before suddenly, a voice at my shoulder asked if the seat beside me was taken. And, Reader, that was exactly how it went.

It was a sunny afternoon towards the end of my trip, the weather was warm, the summer wrapping up in one final golden burst. I was getting a late lunch in a pub near the park when a very good-looking man caught my eye. I caught his back. As if scripted, the seat beside mine became free and over he came. He said his line and I said mine. He asked the question and I said yes. He sat down beside me and we shared a sandwich, drank some beers, talked both like old friends and two people who knew they'd never meet again. After we'd finished eating, I suggested we play pool to decide who paid for the drinks. We were both terrible and that didn't matter. We didn't know the rules, which only made it funnier.

It was easy because we both knew that we wouldn't be keeping in touch, and in that moment, that felt like the most romantic part. We were two single people from opposite sides of the world who were choosing to spend this time together for no other reason than why not? It was a romantic excursion from the normal, predictable run of things and for one single, shining afternoon I was able to forget about the emails that needed to be answered, the bills that nagged to be paid, the long flight back home that would surely end in days of miserable jet lag. Those things faded and shrunk. And when it was time for us both to go it wasn't heartbreaking. He paid for the drinks, I said thank you and we left the bar. We walked together to the park and then kissed on the corner near his train station. As an afterthought, he told me his name and I told him mine. We kissed once more, then said goodbye.

I walked back to my hotel in the bright golden light of evening, beaming at every single person I passed. I felt lighter than I had in weeks, happy and bold and chosen, as though I'd been anointed by some passing romantic sprite. The world around me felt changed too. It was no longer too noisy, too full and too complicated to understand. It was an uncomplicated place full of good, interesting and spontaneous people.

I should have left it at that – the romantic four hours that was never meant to be any more than that, the perfect afternoon that had helped to reignite my belief in these good and spontaneous moments. I didn't, though. Curiosity got the better of me and when I got back to the hotel, I looked him up on social media. A lot of his photos were of scenery, meals, his band rehearsing. And peppered among them were dozens and dozens of pictures of him with his long-term girlfriend, who was waiting for him in a different city. Anniversary posts. Public declarations of enduring love, celebration, monogamy, fidelity, their perfect future, their beautiful life. I closed my phone and flopped onto my hotel bed. Just like that, my perfect, romantic, cinematic afternoon had blinked entirely out of existence. It was gone. The bantering over the rules of pool, the electric brush of his leg against mine when we sat back down at the bar for just one more drink, the kiss on the corner – all vanished into the ether.

And it wasn't heartbreak or rejection I was feeling; I didn't know this guy and just an hour before had felt content to never see him again. What I felt was loss – not of a person or a future but of a feeling and an experience. It had taken me so long to get here and I didn't want to have shared my sweet romantic afternoon with a cheating scumbag – I wanted him to be the man he'd sold himself as, the single, solo traveller who couldn't help but say hello and find out if I was also a single, solo traveller. I wanted the story to be one I could tell without needing to fudge the details or admit what I'd had a part in.

I left my phone lying where it was on the bed and went and got a beer at the hotel bar. I sat out on the terrace and looked down at the city sprawled below, the buildings and roads draped in a fading orange light. And sip by sip, moment by moment, the romance of that day crept back towards me. I realised that it didn't really matter who he'd turned out to be because I had acted within my own values. I had taken the leap without needing to lie and knowing that felt good. I had smiled across the room at a stranger, had told him that he should sit down, had invited him to help himself to the fries that had arrived with my sandwich that I was too full to tackle alone – and I'd do it all again. The romance of that day wasn't contained within him – it was contained in me. It was mine for the keeping and nobody could change that or take it from me. This felt like defiance. This felt like freedom.

Since then, I've tried to hold onto this feeling, tried to maintain this ethos and attitude.

It's important to remember that you can't control other people but you can control your own actions. You alone get to decide if you're going to take the leap, try something new, speak up when it would be easier to say nothing. You can send the message and pick up the phone, be honest about your feelings and let the chips fall. You can get up after being knocked to the ground and instead of reaching for self-flagellation or unkindness, you can take intentional loving care of yourself. You can keep stoking the romance in your life, holding your belief in it close and refusing to let it go.

A romantic life doesn't need to look like a cheesy Hollywood film. It only needs to include your own bravery and boldness, a willingness to try, to reach out a hand across a dark gulf, to say 'sorry', 'thank you' or 'I don't have all the answers, but I want to figure them out together.' That's what love is, I think. It's one gesture with loving intent and then another gesture with loving intent, and another, and another, all linked together like daisies in a chain. It's trying even though it would be easier to sit still, to stay safe, to remain alone, alive but not really living. To live well is to open yourself up to humiliation, to unreturned feelings, to the word 'no', to absolutely no words at all. But it is worth it. It's the best of what we can do together. And so, when a great date doesn't lead anywhere or when someone you invested in turns out to be cruel, try to hold on tight to the fact that you can only ever control your own actions, your own commitment to showing up and trying your best.

Raising your standards and being single is always more romantic than settling for breadcrumbs

It's so easy to get swept up in the fantasy of love as something you must win the hard way, that going through hell to find that happily ever after you've always been chasing makes it more real and long lasting than if it arrives quietly and calmly. It's a story that's familiar to most of us, a refrain we've heard time and time again. Women especially are invited to endure hard times in love, to stay loyal, to hold tighter, to love enough for both people in the relationship. Punishment is coded into our formative romantic journeys.

So, when you meet someone when you're least expecting it, like everyone has always said you will, you'll pay attention. And if, after a great first date, an even better second date and a dizzyingly good third date, even though there are a few red flags, you'll ignore them. Because when things are good, they're really good. You stay up late talking about difficult things – your childhood angers, your secret anxieties, your sexual fantasies – all exchanged as easily as if you were telling each other what you had for lunch. It will make a kind of sense, this intimacy, something in your body drawing towards something in their body. They won't always reply to your texts but after a few weeks they'll introduce you to their friends and you'll be so pleased about it that even though they don't speak to you for most of the night, you'll tell yourself that it doesn't matter – it only matters that they invited you at all, that they obviously like you enough to want you to be a part of their life. When they don't text for a day, you'll tell yourself it's fine, they're just busy with work, with moving house, with this family obligation, that friend in need. You'll buy them a bottle of wine and a jar of overpriced artisanal honey anyway – honey being a traditional Scottish housewarming gift – and wait to be invited over.

And when this doesn't happen, when they cancel on you half an hour before you're meant to meet up, you'll reason that they're just tired, tell yourself that it's fine, plans change, moving is stressful, it's nothing to worry about. And you'll go on saying this for far longer than you should, until it's no longer a day between texts but several days, when it's no longer a bad excuse but no excuse at all. And by the time you realise that it isn't fine, it isn't nothing, it'll be too late. You'll have only a choice between two – sit and wait for it to happen or make it happen yourself. And so, you'll tell them that this isn't fair, isn't fun, that you're out, that you wish them luck.

And for a while you're proud of yourself, your strong resolve, your decisiveness. But then after a few months they start texting again, always late at night. Mostly single words, only occasionally more.

And one night you'll text back. The only time you'll talk about your feelings for one another is when you're both drinking. One weekend, you'll drink too much and when they ask to see you, you'll say yes and they'll tell you they're on their way, that they'll message when they're outside. The next day, their hangover will be a bad one and they'll nap on your chest while you stroke their hair. When they feel better, they'll come and sit outside with you and your friends and it'll be oddly easy. You'll remember what it is you liked so much about them in the first place. They'll get along so well with the people you love most and you'll think, *maybe this time it could be something*. When they leave to go home, you'll make tentative plans and for just a little while, you'll let yourself look forward to them. But then they'll cancel, rearrange, flake on you and it will feel so familiar.

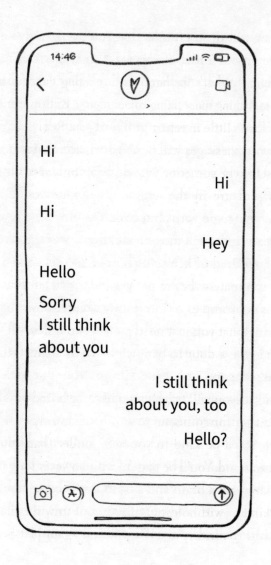

They will drop crumbs that you know aren't enough to live on but a part of you will think, *what's the harm in pretending? What's the harm in just eating these for a while until something more filling comes along?* But opening your heart for so little in return will hurt you. Replying to these one-word messages will be an admission that you believe yourself to be someone who deserves only very little, who finds pleasure in the withholding, who wouldn't even know what to do with abundance.

The months will pass, the texts will stay the same and you'll get tired of it. You'll realise that this person is not your soulmate – they're not even your friend. This situation is not complex or interesting, you see now, not full of potential that you just need patience to unlock. It is dull, a dead end, a door to bang your hands against until you choose to stop.

And so, you will teach yourself to be bored of it, bored of waiting for someone to call or text, only ever late at night. You'll be kind to yourself, kinder than you think you can stand. You'll be patient with however long it takes, knowing that a brain and a heart can become hooked on this kind of withholding, this kind of unwinnable game. You will remind yourself again and again just how dull this is, how devoid of promise, how colourless, how unromantic. It's you picking the petals off a flower – *they like me, they don't like me, they like me, they don't* – trying to arrive at the answer you want until there's nothing lovely left, on and on and on, until eventually . . . *enough*.

Enough of holding your breath. Enough of your heart lighting up only when your phone screen does, of reading and re-reading the same messages over and over, hoping for them to reveal some deeper, hidden meaning. They don't.

Because when the only thing keeping things interesting and alive is your own effort, it's time to let it grow dim and die.

You'll remind yourself that you were taught a lot that wasn't true about love and are now having to unlearn it: films and books portraying it as calamitous, destructive, dramatic; a permanent uncertain feeling, a space inside you only filled when you're near the object of your affection. You're learning that these things don't add up to a long and healthy love, that they leech from you, making you feel crazy and codependent and deserving of only very little.

But real love is lighter and easier. It is abundant and so

long as you're alive and you feel called to go out and look for it, there is every chance you can have it. You aren't a bird eating crumbs, you're a human being and you're hungry. You are a point shining bright on the map. The day is not lost, the journey not over, not even when your blood is heavy or your heart drops like a stone in a pond and you realise that the person you've been feeling so excited about is letting you down and pulling back, that they're not *the one*, they're just *someone*.

You will stop thinking about them so much. You will come home to yourself, realising that you don't want to be destroyed by love after all, that the love you grew up truly, *truly* believing in wasn't a tornado or a knife-edge. The love you want is a soft answer to a hard question, an open door into the world. And so, you will delete and block their number because it's enough now, it really and truly is. It's not a punishment or a low-blow or a last-ditch attempt for their attention and their affection, it's just an exhalation at the appropriate time, the end of a story that has become suddenly so boring and perhaps always was. And gradually, you'll stop hoping they'll find a way to message you or that you'll bump into them with a fresh haircut on a date with someone much taller and far more good looking. You'll feel a little bit sad when you think of what you put up with but it's not a sadness that lingers. You'll nurture a bright bloom of hope for better to come. You'll eat the honey that you bought for them, and it will be so, so sweet.

Romanticising dating doesn't mean ignoring reality

When we model our romantic fantasies on what we've seen on television or in films, we can sometimes forget to let reality in. If someone is charming, funny or good looking enough, we might prioritise our feelings over the facts, ignoring their behaviour in favour of the pretty words they use and the way they (sometimes) make us feel. After years of being let down and disappointed, single and kind of bored, it's all too easy to give in to chemistry and excitement, to let the facts slip away. It might even feel romantic.

A few years ago, I went on a long weekend to Paris with three of my best friends. It was early January, and everything felt ripe and full of promise as our Eurostar glided into Gare du Nord. I was newly single after a string of doomed situationships with chronically flaky guys, and I felt unburdened and excited. It felt apt to be beginning a new year like this – single, empowered and on an adventure. I felt full of a kind of expansive, inflating joy and love for my friends; I almost always had a wine glass in one hand and a disposable camera in the other. The four of us piled into photo booths, giggled quietly at ugly antiques in dusty second-hand shops, and ate and drank as though it was our last weekend on earth. I refused to take off my jauntily angled beret and kept confidently gesturing towards things that were not the Eiffel Tower and saying 'there it is, ze Eiffel Tower' in a silly French accent – offensive to the entire nation of France and potentially even parts of Belgium. The sun was buttery yellow, like one from a Monet painting, the air wintry and crisp. I felt really, truly happy. I was content. I was with people who knew me and loved me, and I felt certain that I couldn't need any more than I had.

On the second morning we were there, I got a message on Instagram from a musician whose songs I vaguely knew. The musician told me he was a fan of my work, thought I was interesting, wondered if I'd be up for a coffee sometime. He was older than me, New York-based but often in the UK for work. We messaged back and forth for the rest of that day and all the next, and by the time he asked if I'd like to go for dinner when we were both back in London, I'd had two thirds of a bottle of wine and said yes right away.

Soon we swapped to texting and for the rest of the trip and the next week, my friends teased me whenever they caught me smiling down at my phone. The musician was funny and enthusiastic, praising my wit and my good taste. We had so much in common, he told me, and even though I thought I knew better than to expect a grand love story from a DM slide, I felt quietly giddy about it, lit up by his attention, his many earnest questions about my life, my inspirations, my opinions. If not quite a resounding *yes*, it was at least a solid *maybe*. Maybe more, maybe real, maybe this.

We made plans to meet the following Friday. The week passed painfully but exhilaratingly slowly. He messaged me constantly, sending me pictures from his gigs, telling me he couldn't wait to see me, that he wanted to spend as much time together as possible, that Friday couldn't come soon enough.

When Friday *did* come, however, our time together had narrowed significantly. Instead of an afternoon, a night and a day, he told me that we only had twelve hours together. I was disappointed but I told myself that a night together could possibly be even more romantic than a weekend, more precious because of how fleeting it would be. I told him where to meet me – a cosy pub with fireplaces, flickering candles and low ceilings. I got there a little early to give myself time to get composed. Seated in a quiet corner, I opened my phone to a text that said he was running late.

By the time he got there, I'd finished a glass of wine and was starting on my second. I was flushed and nervous as he kissed me on both cheeks, sat down beside me and apologised profusely for his lateness. He was earnest and charming about it, and I felt comfortable with him immediately. We ordered some more drinks, talked like we'd known one another for years, seamlessly slipping from one topic to the next, asking and answering questions rapidly, laughing easily. As the night wore on, we made more excuses to bridge the space between us and touch. We ordered more drinks and some food – a burger that I could barely touch because I was so engrossed in our conversation.

But despite this – our chemistry and the excitement of his physical proximity – I was growing more and more anxious. I'd let myself imagine that the hundreds of messages and the hours of flirting were adding up to something greater and more momentous than just one date. I thought this would be obvious upon meeting, that the fairytale would slot into place, that it would be clear to us both that there was more here than one fun night together. But it wasn't obvious at all. My excitement to meet him was quickly morphing into panic about how short our time together was. When he'd said hello, I was already thinking of his goodbye.

I kept the conversation light and smiled a lot, trying to mask any unease. I drank quickly and too much, ignoring the tug of discomfort inside me, the quiet voice that was imploring me to lay my cards on the table and ask if we'd just been flirting or if he really did see something more between us. I didn't, though, not yet secure or confident enough within myself to do this, not aware that it was even allowed. The way I'd felt when I was in Paris – confident, bold, ballsy – became shadowy and distant, a brief costume I'd put on instead of the truth of who I could genuinely be. So, I stayed quiet, laughed at his jokes and swallowed my worries, chasing them with tequila and lime juice. I didn't know then what I would come to know deeply across the next few years of my life, which is that the romantic potential of my life lies within me and my own power, and not inside somebody else.

After dinner, we walked back to my place, only stopping to kiss under streetlights. After we slept together, he fell quickly asleep, snoring softly while I lay awake beside him, unsettled and restless. I imagined our time together nearing its end, fading into nothing, the minutes spilling out like sand. The thing I'd been waiting for and daydreaming about was almost over.

I slept fitfully and woke before the sun was up, finding him already sitting up in bed stroking my hair. I let him touch me like that, telling me in a soft voice about his work, his plans, his journey back to the States, not asking me anything in return. As he rested his cheek against my stomach in the dim and forgiving light of pre-dawn, I considered one last time telling him how I was feeling, telling him that his actions and words hadn't quite lined up and I was disappointed. I took a deep breath in and then released it. There was no point.

And then it was really morning, the room full of white, winter light. The opportunity to speak honestly felt left behind in the dark. He got dressed, hunting out his socks and checking train times, then followed me downstairs so I could unlock the door and let him out. In the doorway he kissed me quickly, told me to stay cool and then left without a single glance back.

As I stood there, my cheeks burning with a confusing and unearned shame, I wanted nothing more than to go upstairs and get back into my unmade bed, pulling the covers over my head and sleeping until noon. But I didn't do that. Instead, I took a long, hot shower, stripped the sheets from my bed, put on a pair of black jeans and my yellowest jumper and took myself out for a walk.

Walking is what I've always done when my heart feels

blue and bruised, and it never fails to make me feel at least the tiniest bit better. I don't go walking to escape my sadness or my disappointment or my fear – but rather to take all my feelings out of the house and into new territory, somewhere other than the confines of my bedroom. I walk to bring my sorrow and confusion out into the light and the fresh air, where they, and I, are always welcome to be. It is a small but reliable way to bring an otherwise uncomfortable and disappointing day a little more under my control.

I bought myself a foamy, sweet coffee at the end of my road and with each sip, and each step, I felt just a little bit restored, a little more at home with myself. I took my usual route through the park – two loops around the bowling green, once across the bridge to look for fish in the little stream, through the garden with the fountain, stopping under the pergolas to see if there were any nesting birds, and then to the bench that looks downhill towards the main road. Once there, I drank the rest of my coffee, watching dogs chasing one another around, the pink-cheeked children collecting leaves to show their tired but proud parents, the couples walking arm in arm, hands in each other's back pockets.

As I sat there, I realised that I will always have a choice about what to do and what story to tell. I realised that I could, if I decided, build a miserable narrative around this night and this man, casting myself in the role of a jilted and tragic figure and the musician as a cruel and careless stranger. Or I could decide otherwise. I could dust off, chalk this situation up to miscommunication and mismatched expectations, and take whatever lessons there were to be learned. I could opt to be kind to myself, allowing any embarrassment or disappointment to dissipate while I got on with my life.

I walked back towards home, telling myself the reassuring things that I'd tell any one of my friends who found themselves in a similar situation – that it was okay to be disappointed but that it was not the end of the world that this wouldn't become any more than a chance meeting; that sometimes what you think is going to be dizzyingly romantic ends up feeling only like play-acting excitement and romance. I told myself that life can remain romantic and full even when there is some disappointment and dashed hope; that each of us can stay loving and hopeful even when things fail to turn out exactly as planned or imagined.

And this is true – it couldn't be truer. When hard things happen you always have a choice: you can send your love towards your fear and turn it into bravery, or you can starve it, ignore it, pretend it isn't happening. You can choose to feel the fear and the uncertainty all around you and still choose to act, to reach out. You can express your needs to the person in front of you and then let them choose to meet them or not meet them. And if it's a no, then that's information you need, information that can bolster you and show you how brave you can be, how much real love and an equal partnership matters to you.

The world is big and busy and bright and ever-changing. A crush that doesn't evolve into love really doesn't matter in the grand scheme of things. The romance and magic of your life is not contained in someone else but within you, and you can build beauty and romance into reality, instead of just telling a pretty story and hoping someone else arrives to make it come true. If you whole-heartedly get busy building a beautiful life – a genuinely romantic life – then eventually it will not be 'stay cool' and a closed door, it will be 'I think you're so cool, and I would love to see you again.' Believe that. Believe that and get to work.

Heartbreak and rejection

It's never easier to romanticise your life when things are going well in your love life and never more difficult than when they're crashing down around you. When you're heartbroken – dumped or cheated on, or just at the end of the road with someone you've been seeing – the world around you can take on a cruel tint, a dullness that no amount of positive thinking or self-care can brighten up. When this happens it's okay if you're not able to snap out of it, not able to use romanticising to lift yourself free of sadness or grief. Moving on from a relationship or a person takes time, and it's time that you can give yourself.

And once the darkest clouds have passed and you feel a little better, here are some tips on romanticising dating after heartbreak and not letting fears or feelings of rejection overwhelm you:

When someone tells you they're not looking for something serious, always, always believe them

We set ourselves up for so much unnecessary rejection and pain when we decide that we could be the special exception for an unavailable but alluring person, that if we just show our very best sides then they'll change their minds and want us. Doing this is unfair both to us and to them. It positions their expressed wants and needs as less important than our desire for them. As much as we all root for the fairytale, it isn't romantic to ignore reality, to chase and chase someone who has already been upfront about what they can and can't offer. Accept what they're saying and go elsewhere, to where something real could grow.

Remind yourself that rejection is rarely personal

It isn't a slight on your character when someone doesn't feel the same spark or want the same things that you want. Physical and emotional attraction is a strange and unpredictable magic, and it's incredibly cruel and self-punishing to decide that every failed connection is somehow your fault or evidence of something that you're lacking. In dating, we will be gently knocked back and we will do the same to others. Sometimes, objectively wonderful, funny, cool people who seem perfect for us won't be meant for us at all, and when that happens there's nothing to do but wish them well and move on.

Work on your sensitivity to rejection

If it feels like a problem or a destructive force, then it deserves your attention and your time. You can do this alone or with a therapist. It doesn't mean you need to eradicate it entirely or shame yourself for feeling it, but rather take a closer look at what triggers it and how you respond when you feel it. What is your response when you feel a sense of rejection? Do you self-isolate or start internalising, or are you able to call a friend or choose a more constructive reaction? Do you have any reassuring affirmations in place for when you need to support yourself through rejection? Are you able to greet rejection and sadness at things not working out with acceptance and neutrality instead of judging the feelings themselves? When you're better able to tolerate disappointment and sadness, and sit in discomfort, you're better able to take romantic risks and really put yourself out there, which is ultimately what it takes to have that big love that you may be looking for.

Practise gratitude

Dating contains so many lovely/cute/sexy/exciting/spontaneous moments and it pays to notice them. Instead of trying to predict the future, be present. So much of the joy of dating and love is lost in our worries about whether things will always be that good, that sexy, that charged, that effortless. Instead of living in the glow of the moment, we instead worry over what will change, when it will change and how it might all come crashing down around us. For the anxiously attached among us, it can be a struggle but getting out of our own heads and into a more secure and mindful place is possible. Because when you're worrying about someone else's opinion of you, your life itself narrows to a small and miserable point. When you dwell on how short a phone call was or whether your date seemed a little iffy about making plans to visit your grandma's llama farm in the spring, you're not really living. So instead, when things are good – when you're smiling at a text or holding their hand or kissing in the rain – say a quiet thank you to the Universe. That's what dating and love and life are all about.

When a relationship ends, keep a souvenir

Not a lock of their hair or a pair of their pants, but something about them that you really treasured. Keep a shared private joke as a kind of memento or try to implement something that they taught you into your everyday life. If they were the kind of person who stopped to properly read all the plaques at a museum or gallery, who petted every cat they saw, who complimented strangers with ease, who baked for neighbours, try doing these things yourself. Remain close and keep the best of them with you even as you move on and heal.

DATING YOURSELF

There's a long running joke among my single friends that one of the only reasons we invite our dates to come over these days is because it gives us the motivation to tidy our rooms. We're (mostly) kidding of course but there is an element of truth in the punchline. Love, or even just a crush, can be a galvanising force – electric, active and lifegiving. When we want to impress a new person, we automatically work harder at being our own best selves – funnier, sexier, flirtier, more engaging, more closely connected with our interests and hobbies. We take longer to do our hair and our makeup; we think ahead about what we want to wear instead of throwing on the closest and cleanest pair of jeans.

The problem here is that when the object of our interest is gone, this motivation and drive towards self-improvement can wane too, dislodging us from our starry-eyed orbit and bringing us back down to earth, back to who we were before we felt that other pair of eyes observing us. Often our disappointment at the end of a fling or a crush isn't because we'll miss the person's presence or proximity in our life, but because we'll miss who we felt ourselves becoming in our desire to be chosen by them, the new and better life that seemed so tantalisingly within reach.

But perhaps there's a way to capture and redirect that feeling, to feel like you're dating even when you're not, to focus that electric and vital energy not on some stranger, but on yourself. In the last few years, I've gone from tentatively trying it out – this practice where I consistently and without irony treat myself like my own lover – to making it a fundamental part of my routine. I take myself out, seek new experiences, go to gigs and sit in theatres all alone. I handle myself with the loving care, affection and admiration and intrigue that I have for my romantic partners. I tell my friends that I'm dating myself and I mean it.

This practice of dating yourself comes with its own set of learning curves, though. The first time I took myself out for dinner alone for 'no reason', beyond having no plans and trying to convince myself I deserved it, I burned and squirmed with embarrassment, totally convinced that every other diner in the restaurant had judgemental eyes on me, mocking my one set of cutlery, my one wine glass, the empty chair on the other side of the table. I was certain they were thinking all sorts of mean or pitying thoughts. My brain was still trained to go right to the unkindest interpretations, and so it didn't occur to me until much later how unlikely it was that they cared at all. Much more likely was that they were either busy enjoying their meals and hadn't even noticed me or had been only briefly curious as to my aloneness before forgetting about me entirely the minute their food arrived. I felt the same kind of twisting shame when I started going to the cinema alone, even though there were plenty of other people by themselves there too, even though we had all gone with the same intention of literally sitting in the darkness and watching a movie in silence.

Planning solo 'date nights' at home also made me self-conscious. Making a lone cocktail and cooking an elaborate meal for one felt odd, almost pointless. I kept asking myself *Why am I doing this? What's the occasion?*

I told myself that I should be boiling the kettle for a Pot Noodle instead, scrolling enviously through other people's fun Instagram stories in front of some trashy TV before having an early night. Any more was too much for one. Any more was undeserved.

But I kept at it. I kept going to restaurants or cafes and ordering meals just for me. My book, headphones, journal and pen felt like armour against judgement, amulets of protection. I kept browsing the showtimes at local cinemas, sitting in the dark with my overpriced popcorn and the sweets I smuggled in. I kept cleaning the entire

flat on Friday and then planning a favourite meal or a new recipe to try, lighting fresh candles and thinking about what album to put on the record player, even though I knew my flatmate was out and it would only be me there for the evening.

It was a while before it became easy, even longer before it came fully enjoyable, but I did notice that there was a kind of power that grew every time I sat somewhere alone or kept to my plans to do something nice by and for myself. I persisted for two reasons: the first was because of my own deeply rooted stubbornness – I wanted to get this right; the second was a growing sense that something in my interior world really needed to change.

For so long, doing things for my own joy was something that had repelled me, had represented excess and frivolity, and that was something I wanted to overcome. Though I enjoyed being single and wasn't dependent on a romantic relationship for happiness, I noticed that my self-esteem wobbled after every bad date and took a hit with even the littlest knockback. Subconsciously, I knew I was waiting for a second person to arrive at the threshold of my life and make it exciting for me, to make me into a real person worthy of sensation and pleasure. After years of this same, sad dance, I was tired. I wanted to do it myself.

Dating yourself requires patience, a tolerance for minor discomforts and a willingness to try again and again until things start to feel easier. I've learned that dating yourself isn't all that different from dating other people – you think about when you're free, what you'd most like to do, where you could go after if things are going well and you're having a good time. You anticipate it in the days before, looking forward to your meal, your cocktails or the show you've been dying to see. You get yourself ready and you let it take time. You shower and wash and style your hair. You wear something that you feel great in and you take a moment to really admire yourself in the mirror, maybe giving yourself a heartfelt compliment on your way out of the door. You go out and you make a proper effort to enjoy yourself, your own company, the world around you. You maybe spend a little more money than you might usually because it is, after all, a special occasion. You show up. You give it your all. You see how it feels.

Of course, dating yourself is not quite the same experience as dating another human person. There's less in the way of conversation and fewer set rules – it would be perfectly acceptable, for example, to get somebody else's number while on a date with yourself, whereas it's mostly frowned upon if you're out on a date with another person! But there can still be a similar sense of occasion, a familiar happy feeling at the end, a knowledge that you grew closer to the person who you were spending time with and learned more about them.

Dating yourself, whether you want to call it that or not, is you demonstrating that you are worth real and sustained effort and thoughtfulness – that you don't have to be partnered up to deserve space in the world. The opera, the cinema, the beach, the park, a hotel, a fancy bar, your local pub, a candlelit French bistro – nothing is off limits for you and their romance is not only unlocked when you pair up.

MORE TIPS FOR DATING YOURSELF:

Take things slowly

Begin with activities that you're already familiar with, activities that you can tweak to make them feel like a little bit more of an occasion. For example, instead of going to your usual multiplex to see a movie, you could take a trip to one of those fancy cinemas where you can eat a gourmet hot dog and drink a big glass of wine or a cocktail while sitting in an enormous comfy armchair. If you're a cyclist, you could plan a particularly scenic bike ride followed by a solo picnic with cordials and cake and a book. If you normally spend your Sunday sitting in a cafe on your phone, you could go a little further afield to a slightly more upmarket place, order an elaborate frothy coffee or a hot chocolate and a stack of pastries, and stake out the best seat in the place for a long morning of doing the crossword and reading.

You can even plan a 'date night' that doesn't take too much planning or spending: a nice bottle of wine, your favourite takeaway and that expensive candle that you got for Christmas and for some reason haven't gotten around to lighting. Some of my favourite days in the last few years have been those where I took myself out on purpose and treated myself as though I was my own love interest.

Remember: you don't always need an occasion
Get yourself treats and gifts without needing a particular reason why. So many of us wouldn't hesitate for a single

moment before buying something for a loved one – maybe they had a rough week or got some bad news, or maybe you just saw something and it made you think of them. You send flowers, a cute handwritten postcard, a little ceramic frog wearing tiny dungarees because of an in-joke that's been running for a decade, a Pot Noodle, a packet of novelty condoms, fancy chocolates that you know they love but wouldn't buy themselves. And yet when it comes to doing the same for yourself, you falter and stall, talk yourself out of that lovely bath bomb that's on sale or that packet of sweets in the corner shop, even though you haven't had them in years and you know they'll conjure up so much nostalgic joy the minute you put one into your mouth. Your hand moves past the slightly nicer bottle of wine on the shelf to something cheaper; you put back the special edition copy of the book in favour of getting the eBook. But this is no way to live, not on this finite planet in these finite bodies.

Certainly, you don't need to give into every urge and follow every whim – it's not the least bit romantic to live beyond your means and put yourself in the danger of debt – but you do need

to give yourself some permission to treat yourself as though you're entirely worthy of small pleasure. (NB: As I mentioned earlier in the book, I don't advocate for mass overconsumption. But small treats and indulgences are another matter entirely, and one I'm in full support of.) We're only here for so long, so do treat yourself.

Don't flake

Whenever possible, make and keep your plans for a solo date. Decide how frequently would be reasonable for you and your circumstance – perhaps with young children or other responsibilities you simply don't have the time at present to go out for a meal alone or get out of the house for anything but errands or work, for more than forty-five minutes. But where possible, try to make it a habit and an ongoing practice – something you mark with a heart on the calendar and stick with, just as you would a date night with another person.

Simple plans can be lovely too

A solo date could be an early morning walk on a beautiful day around the park, a stroll around a Sunday market or a

brunch where you reserve your favourite table and catch up on all your favourite podcasts. It certainly could be an evening of fine dining, a day of spa pampering or a stay in a nice hotel, but it doesn't need to be for it to be valuable or a part of your romantic practice. Leave the house and breathe the fresh air! Buy an ice cream and smile at a hottie! It's all good, worthwhile stuff.

Don't stop dating yourself when you start dating someone else

Though more of your time may be spent doing lovely things with your partner, it remains important that you continue to show yourself love and care, that your needs are not only met by other people. Your own company is still plenty good enough and your independence is intact. So, carve out evenings alone, little hobbies and habits that are just for you, moments of peace where you can do precisely as you please.

Treat your relationship with yourself as though it matters – because it really does

It's like any other connection – it requires effort, patience, love, forgiveness, playfulness. And if frustration or problems arrive, you can address those as you would if they had come up between you and a partner – by facing them and trying to make things better. The relationship that you have with yourself is a relationship that you will be in for the rest of your life, so prioritise and protect it.

THE APPS CAN BE YOUR ALLY
OR YOUR ENEMY

It's easy to forget how new dating apps are. They're so endemic, so woven into so much of the current social and romantic landscape, that it can be a bit of a shock to remember that only a decade or so ago most of them were only just launching. There's an expectation to use them, to not make a fuss and just sign up, letting an algorithm point you in the direction of swarms of strangers who may or may not send you the aubergine emoji with a winking face and four question marks.

I was at university around the time that these apps became commonplace and I dutifully downloaded Tinder with my friends. We were all hooked at once, swiping obsessively for weeks, fascinated by this new technology, a gateway into the world of love, sex and romance. Before that, we had to go out of our student halls to meet potential dates, brushing by them at parties or trying to catch their eye across club dance floors. It seemed magical, miraculous. Nowadays, it can feel more like a chore.

There's a fatigue regarding these apps that single people often speak about. Using them can be tiring, impersonal, sometimes even downright degrading. I downloaded the apps initially with hopefulness and real curiosity, but after years of accruing matches, being verbally sexually harassed and making endless small talk, they sometimes feel more like an enemy than an ally in the search for a great relationship and an epic romance.

When dating is reduced to algorithms and monthly fees it can be tempting to get carried off into your daydreams, imagining what could happen, where things could go. Your thoughts stray away from the present, away from what is really happening – the uncertainty and the app that wants you to spend £29.99 a month for access to a disappointing list of local singles who might deign to stand you a glass of wine and sleep with you once but definitely won't call you after. You bypass reality and land somewhere in a false and far-off future. You have a good date and imagine the next one and the next one and the one after that. You suffer a hilarious mishap together and think about it becoming a shared joke that only the two of you understand. They text late at night to say that they're thinking about you, and you tell yourself it means that they can't be without you. You get bored on your commute and look at their pictures beside yours, wondering what your children might look like.

Often, it's harmless, but done too regularly it becomes a way to escape the present moment and skip ahead to what feels like the better part of the story. And in doing this you miss the magic of the early days, the sparkle of the little moments while you're getting to know a new person.

A few years ago, I went through a terrible, horrible breakup, a breakup that (at the time) felt like the end of the world. It was with a guy I'd been with for a couple of years and though we loved one another, we had reached the end of the road, I felt it had become too much of a mess and it felt long past the point of being able to fix things between us. Things ended in the spring of 2018. Shortly after that, I moved out of the flat we shared and into a house on the other side of London with three close friends.

Healing was hard going, with a lot of breaking down, tearful weekly therapy sessions, blocking and unblocking his number, hoping he would call, hoping he would not. Eventually, the seemingly impossible happened – I felt better. By then, it was the height of summer and the weather in the UK was scorching. The England football team were still doing well in the World Cup and the city felt alive with a kind of flirtatious, anything-could-happen energy. I was still relearning how to be single after two years in a serious relationship and so I downloaded a buffet of dating apps to help my transition. At first, I attended to them with care, thoughtfully creating profiles that seemed honest but showed my best sides, letting potential matches know I could be funny and easy-going, but that I had real depth too. I thought about my interests and my dating goals, trying to communicate my sense of mischief without seeming to lack depth or intelligence.

It only took a few weeks before my attitude changed completely. It was too easy to use these apps for a quick fix of validation or a plea for sexual or romantic attention. I found myself turning to them whenever I was bored at work, on public transport or struggling to sleep. I dragged my thumb this way and that way, over and over again, by then just searching for a dopamine hit instead of any kind of proper connection. I suppose it was the promise and the potential of an imagined person that I was looking for, rather than the real, intentional and difficult work of a proper relationship. I wanted to be wanted, in other words. I wanted to be hungry more than I wanted to be fed.

After a couple of months of having very few (read: zero) meaningful interactions, I had to face myself and look more closely at how I was behaving. In my haste to move on from the breakup, and the shattering of a once-treasured relationship, I'd made dating into a game, treating my matches like characters inside a console instead of real people. I'd drained all the romance and promise out of dating until it was just pixels, empty prompts, attraction by numbers, pointless swiping. I was collecting fellow human beings like Pokémon cards, and even in my heartbroken and healing state I knew that wasn't fair.

It's so easy to fall into this pattern. So much of modern living centres around convenience. If we can't do it quickly and via our smart phone, then why bother at all? But love and true human connection is not a matter of expediency. It takes work to build a bond and care to preserve it, not just a few clicks and well-chosen pickup lines.

And so, not long after my disastrous debut back onto the apps, I knew I needed to rein things in and make some tweaks. I deleted all but one of these apps from my phone and vowed to no longer use it late at night or in states of boredom or agitation – which, I've learned, is like going to the supermarket while you're hungry. I tried instead to operate with greater care, only matching with a few people at a time and then making the effort to talk to them properly before deciding if I wanted to go on a date or just wish them luck and keep it moving. I tried to resist the urge to make snap judgements before I'd really given people a chance. All of this resulted in yielding connections that were deeper and outcomes that felt far more positive.

Still, romanticising these apps is easier said than done. Even when you yourself are on your best behaviour, they can often feel like cold and unwelcoming places, leaving so much room for small abandonments, unanswered questions and countless indignities. Sometimes a person you've been getting along great with will go quiet out of the blue, their profile disappearing completely, leaving you unsure if you've been unmatched or if the person just deleted the app. There's also the constant prompting by the apps to spend money to unlock more features – greater numbers of singles in your area, a better chance of being seen by the most in demand accounts. After a few weeks or months of use, you can feel burned out and act on autopilot, with the availability of seemingly limit-less new matches turning even the most romantic and patient among us into dopamine-seeking robots, swiping without thinking, matching without care. This is the antithesis of romantic living – careless, impersonal and against our best interests in the long term.

When you're on the apps and meeting people it can help to remind yourself that you're one half of every conversation you're having and every date you go on, and you can't expect from others what you refuse to offer yourself. You've got to show up, not just in body but in heart and intention, giving people a chance to show you who they are before you judge them as untrustworthy or lacking in some way.

MORE WAYS TO MAKE THE APPS YOUR ALLY

Take frequent breaks

These apps can be so fun in the beginning with the initial excitement of seeing dozens and dozens of potential romances. But scrolling every day for weeks and failing to meet anyone can somewhat take the shine and romance off dating. A normal consequence of this is a sense of burnout and disconnect from other people, so instead of using the apps like they're going out of style – human-window shopping and swiping like you're trying to get jam off your phone screen – try to intentionally slow your roll. Be proactive on them for a week or two and then give yourself a period of rest when you stay off them completely. This can also be a good chance to exchange numbers with some of the people you've been talking to or make plans to actually meet up.

Try not to be discouraged by other people's bad behaviour – it's just them revealing who they are

If someone is rude or sexist, or creepy or dismissive on the apps just unmatch them and spare them no more than a crumb of your pity before taking a deep breath and moving on. It certainly doesn't mean there's not infinitely better things ahead. Try not to draw a correlation between one bad experience and all future romantic potential.

Accept that it can be a boring process

App dating won't be all hilarious and sexy back-and-forth chats with sexy singles in your area. Most of the people you talk to on dating apps won't feel familiar or custom built for you, won't pique your interest or have your heart racing. And do you know what? That's fine. It's totally normal! These are just strangers who are on the same quest that you're on – trying to find their person, fall in love, have fun sex – and them liking or not liking you has no bearing on what romance lies in store for either of you.

Try not to make snap decisions but equally, don't be afraid to trust your instincts

If you sense that a person or situation is simply not for you, go with it. You don't always need justifications for a mismatch. If it feels wrong that's reason enough.

Know what your non-negotiables are

Not their height or style or how much like Harry Styles or Dev Patel or Kenny from Killing Eve they look, but who they are, how they navigate conflict, how they speak to and about you, how they speak to and about others, what their values include and what kind of life they seek to live. Have an idea of what doesn't work for you – e.g. someone who communicates sporadically when you need to talk things through or someone who probably doesn't want children when you've dreamed of parenthood your whole life. You don't have to open conversations with a barrage of questions and proclamations about these non-negotiables, but they can be a helpful guide and way to avoid getting too deep with someone who may not truly be your person.

Let them match your energy

Of course, the other app users aren't there purely to entertain you but they should at least mirror your energy and your interest after a few conversations. And if they don't? So it goes. Not everyone needs to be your perfect other half. Most people you match with will be fine, normal, lovely people who don't give you any kind of heart or trouser tingle. But every so often it goes the other way. That's what you're holding out for – remember that.

Seek out the positives

Online dating means you can meet hotties while sitting on the sofa in your underpants. How amazing is that?!

Enjoy the ease of it and try not to automatically group it in with all the other joyless processes that you do on your phone – calling the GP, following up on emails, checking your bank balance. If it feels that much like a chore then you're not going to want to do it, and if you don't want to do it then it's unlikely to take you anywhere remotely exciting.

Remember that dating apps are just one way to meet people

If, despite your best efforts, you truly hate them then you absolutely don't have use them. To walk away from dating apps can even be a really empowering step, something you do to stay true to yourself. Because even though the apps are everywhere, they're still a relatively new way of dating, made popular by convenience and novelty. Not being a fan of them doesn't count you out of love or make you a weird outlier. They're not the only way to date and to build a loving relationship (no matter what their ad campaigns might suggest) and although they might offer ease and immediacy, they're as fraught with problems as any approach. Do what feels most right for you.

Here are some journal prompts that help to remind you that love and dating can be romantic, and that you're allowed to seek exactly what you want while still finding joy in the process:

Growing up, I believed that love looked like . . .

....
....
....
....
....

Nowadays, I know that real love looks like . . .

....
....
....
....

When I think of true love, the real-life couples that come to mind are . . .

....

....

....

The key features of a good and joyful relationship are . . .

....

....

....

The most romantic gestures someone can make without spending money are . . .

....

....

....

....

The best things about having a crush are . . .

....

....

....

....

....

....

....

Three big lessons I've learned from dating are . . .

....

....

....

....

....

....

....

Some of my favourite songs, poems, films and books about love include . . .

....

....

....

....

....

My non-negotiable traits for a long-term partner are . . .

....

....

....

....

....

....

....

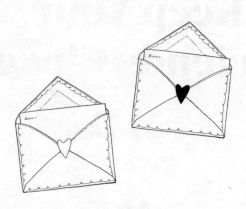

Keep Your
Friends Close

For most of us, it's a no-brainer that the greatest loves of our lives aren't only the people that we date – they're our friends, too. Our mates are our favourite people, the ones who know us best, our companions on the journey of life, our ride or dies. And yet, how often do we really take the time to think of them in that context? How often do we take a moment to gaze at them with starry-eyed gratitude, wondering quite what we did to deserve their presence in our life year after year, through crises and celebrations?

It's okay if the answer is 'not as often as we should'. It's okay if it feels like there are just a few too many messages from old mates that have gone unanswered lately; catchups that have been postponed yet again; meetups, birthday dinners or nights out that have been missed. Adult life can often feel busy and hectic, full of obligation and noise – an ongoing exercise in learning how to juggle and manage and keep your chin above a rising tide. Reconsidering your priorities and tending to your primary relationships in new ways are things that don't need to be driven by shame or self-hatred. There are plenty of ways to romanticise your friendships going forward without beating yourself up for not doing more of it sooner.

We often fail to mark milestones with our close friends because there's less of a social script around it, rather than due to a lack of care or appreciation for the friendship. Instead, the time, money and effort of celebration is mostly reserved for romantic connections, almost all of which do not last a fraction of how long our friendships do. We can spend the greatest portion of life with our friends, have the richest cache of memories and the greatest stories, and yet rarely or never be asked to talk about them, celebrate them publicly, make declarations of joy and commitment.

It seems incredible that we don't do more to celebrate our friendships, considering how vital a role they play. We don't mark anniversaries or send cards each year that say things like, 'On this day when we were six years old, a teacher placed us side by side in line and that was some of the greatest luck of my life.' Or, 'We met in the toilets of the worst club on earth and even though I was trying not to be sick in my bag, you still managed to make me laugh and now I'd give you a kidney.' We let the days pass unnoticed and unmarked instead of shouting from the rooftops about how lucky, how grateful, how happy we are to know them. In this way, we may subtly be treating our friendships as though they're second-tier connections, placeholders for the main event: a romantic relationship.

Among some of the greatest regrets from my early twenties are the ways in which I neglected my friendships while I was trying to work on a relationship or grow a romantic bond with someone I can hardly even recall now. When I look back at the men that I felt infatuated with in my youth, they could be anyone. They're blurs in time, becoming less and less real the closer I try to get to them. But my friends? They are vivid and immediate in my recollections, solid and preserved, as familiar as a film I've watched over and over. I can see long hair flying out of open car windows, hands clasped as we weaved through parties and nightclubs, glitter sparkling under bathroom lighting as we touched up one another's makeup, tearful arguing over something silly and then making up immediately, laughing until we cried, all of us together, growing up and becoming ourselves side by side.

Sometimes it's hard not to feel a mix of regret and curiosity about what might have been different if my attention and time had been more heavily weighted in favour of the people who I already knew and loved: my friends. What wonderful memories might I have made if

I hadn't abandoned that one girls' night halfway through to meet up with a guy at a different party across town? What support would I have received had I leaned on my friends the way they told me time and time again I was allowed to? Whose pain could I have lessened slightly by showing up for my mates with the same unshakeable devotion as I was so used to demonstrating to boyfriends? It isn't that I ever fully neglected anyone, but I made certain leaps and assumptions, believing that there was a kind of inbuilt permanence to these attachments, that they simply didn't need the same care and attention as romantic or familial relationships. *Of course my friends will always be there,* I thought. *Of course these bonds will remain strong and secure no matter what.* I know now that this isn't true, that friendships can be lost, can fade, can be broken. We have to take good and deliberate care of all of our connections and know that none of them are guaranteed to last if we don't make an effort to keep them healthy and ongoing.

This isn't to say you need to dwell on the past, on what you did or didn't do. You can instead make those efforts and improvements now, thinking of how you can romanticise your friendships today – and in the future – in both small and more significant ways. It's not too late, not for

137

any of us. And so, when one of your friends mentions in passing something they like – a favourite flower or ice cream flavour or scent of candle – make a little note of it for future use. When they express anxiety or fear about an upcoming appointment, interview or presentation at work, mark it on your own calendar too, so that you can remember to wish them luck or just send over a particularly silly meme that morning. When they're struggling or grieving or feeling lost, just be there, send a message or a gift, or take yourself to where they are and see how you can help.

It's also a wonderful idea to make time to celebrate and recall all of the important milestones with your friends: when you first met or crossed paths (even if this was long before you actually became close), when you first realised you were the same kind of weird as each other, when you first stayed up all night talking or peed in front of each other without thinking twice about it. You can mark it by going out for cocktails, treating them to a long dinner, cooking for them at home, sending food, flowers, a letter, a gift. Even if it feels a little silly at first, I promise that it isn't something you'll look back at with embarrassment. Because anniversaries aren't just for romantic partners, and we rob ourselves of endless moments of celebration and gratitude when we decide that they are.

Indeed, more and more straight women are now choosing to decentre men and romance, focusing a greater share of their finite energy and time on earth on other things: their careers, their friendships, themselves. They're building big and beautiful lives, the happiness and success of which do not hinge on whether a potential romantic partner does or does not return their affection and attraction. So many of the things we love and value within our friendships are not all that different to the things we love and value in romantic relationships: knowing that someone has your back; having someone to go places with; sharing your dreams and ideas of the future; giving and receiving compliments, affirmations and encouragement; the quiet pleasure of eating a meal together in either comfortable silence or excitable chatter; being each other's secret keeper and witness through life's best and worst moments; being there to remind one another of who you are, where you've been and what you're capable of. Even if you crave romance, a marriage, a family and a traditional relationship, you can still place enormous and well-earned value on other connections.

One night, when I was a teenager, I slipped and fell into a muddy ditch outside of a friend's house. His parents were away overnight and a group of us had been there since the afternoon, drinking cans of weak, lukewarm cider and trying to think of something to do to make the most of the unexpected gift of a free house. It was the school summer holidays but the weather was bad and the mood was tense. The boys in our group were behaving prickly towards us, moody and mean for some unknown teenage boy reason. One friend overheard a cruel and careless comment made about her; another argued with her boyfriend not very quietly in another room. Nobody was having a good time.

Eventually, we stalked outside to loiter near the road – for a bit of fresh air and space and to punish the boys with our absence. We were on a remote country lane that didn't see much traffic and we didn't hear the car until it was almost upon us, tearing too fast around a tight bend. Everyone in the group stumbled backwards at the very same moment that the car whooshed by, but it was only me who lost their balance entirely, falling off the shoddy tarmac of the country road and into a stream of foul-smelling, freezing cold mud. It happened fast: one moment I was dry, wearing my knock-off Ugg boots and skinniest Topshop jeans, and the next I was mid-thigh in shit, my treasured Blackberry (on loan to me by a friend after I had lost my own pink Motorola Razr at a party in a field) sunk forever in the bog, swallowed by sewage, along with a ring I'd scrimped and saved to buy from Pandora and the can of cider I'd been holding.

My friends rallied immediately, swearing at the car as it vanished around the next corner before moving together like a well-trained military unit to rescue me. Several pairs of arms hoisted me up and out, and got me back on my feet. I was ushered back towards the house via the back way so the boys wouldn't see me. One friend hosed me off in the garden, another found me something to change into, another called her mum and sweet-talked her into coming to collect us. I remember with deep fondness how they emptied the cupboard under the sink of shopping bags to lay over the back seat so I wouldn't ruin the interior of the car, how they wound down the window and reassured me that the smell wasn't that bad, that it would definitely come out of my clothes and shoes, how none of the boys had laughed that hard when they'd seen me, how they'd all have forgotten about it the next time we hung out.

Back at my friend's house, I took off the rest of my stinking, sodden clothes at the door, stuffed them into a plastic bag and carefully crept up the stairs to where my friends were running hot water for a bath. For some reason – solidarity or sadness or some other teenage girl impulse – we all squeezed into the tub together, sitting in our pants and bras, emptying and refilling the water until it finally ran clean. We were all in tears by then, crying the way that only teenage girls can cry, sobbing about everything and nothing – mean boyfriends and lost mobile phones and ruined shoes and the apparently unending indignity of being a young woman. We held and reassured each other, fluffed up the bubbles and blew them at one another, wiped at the streaks of cheap mascara and eyeliner that had collected under our eyes and streamed down to our chins. We cried until we were laughing again, and then went on laughing until we forgot we'd been crying at all.

As I've gotten older, I've realised that this is what truly good friendship looks like: being covered in shit and knowing that help is coming, that there's no judgment, that someone will fetch the bin bags, someone will hose you down and someone else will get the towels and the plastic bags, and that all of this will happen without you having to plead or feel embarrassed for even a moment. Truly good friendship is witnessing one another in pain, embarrassed or laid low by life, and just being there, physically and emotionally proximal, until the worst of it has passed and the laughing can resume.

Recently, one of my oldest friends – someone I've known since I was six years old and the one who had been first to hoist me out of the valley of sewage – travelled from Manchester to London to celebrate another friend's birthday. We got ready for the evening together at my flat, trying on one another's clothes and sharing items of makeup while drinking questionable tasting canned margaritas we'd picked up at the corner shop.

Later, after the party, tired and tipsy from dancing in the kitchen and drinking too many negronis, glasses of prosecco and weird apricot liqueur, we giggled our way through parallel bedtime routines, wordlessly handing one another the things we needed – cotton pads, micellar water and moisturiser. We cooked an oven pizza and ate it in bed before cleaning our teeth side by side. In the dim quiet of my bedroom, we lay next to each other, ignoring the crumbs on top of the duvet as our voices and giggles grew softer and softer until, eventually, we fell asleep mid-conversation, just as we used to do when we were little girls having weekend sleepovers.

When she left the next morning, I marvelled at the life that we'd lived together – more than two decades of knowing the very best and the very worst of one another's days, the bright, golden thread that had gone on connecting us no matter how far apart we might have lived or how long it had been between visits, a thread that might stretch and change but that, if I'm lucky, will never break.

Last summer, I was lying on a beach alone. It was a weekday, my day off, and there weren't many other people there. I was fresh and sticky from the sea, leaning in the shade against one of the old wooden groynes, enjoying the sun on my legs, only half concentrating on the book I had brought. It was too hot to wear my bulky headphones and so I had taken them off and was listening to the waves and the gulls and the conversation all around me. A short distance away, an older couple was sitting together under a wide umbrella. I heard the husband grumble to his wife about a group of young girls on the next part of the beach along. I looked over to see them leaning together to take photographs. They were quick and well-practised at it in the way that most teenage girls are, switching from one pose to the next with fluidity, never quite stopping, always in motion, moving their faces from one expres-

sion to the next.

'Why can't they just be here? Why can't they be present?' the man wanted to know. 'They're in this beautiful place and they're just staring at screens.'

I don't think he was speaking from a place of malice, and certainly most of us at one time or another have missed the potential beauty of the here and now by scrolling mindlessly on our phones or taking selfies, instead of sitting, noticing, experiencing. But watching these girls cling to one another, kissing each other's cheeks, laughing as their untied hair mingled together in the sea breeze and obscured one another's faces, I didn't see wasted moments or a lack of presence or potential future regret. I saw a group of young people who were doing their best to be fully and wholly here in one of the ways they'd learned to. They had come to spend the day in a beautiful place and in one another's company, perhaps enjoying the start of an early summer holiday, perhaps taking a day off from revising for exams, perhaps cramming in quality time before they all went off to different universities. They were having fun, laughing, smiling, giving each other compliments as they tapped the phone screen. They were marking the day and making a record of it.

When the taking of the photos was finished – over in a matter of minutes, in fact – they all threw their phones into their beach bags or tucked them underneath towels and then chased each other, laughing and whooping like little children, into the cold salt water. It was clear they loved one another deeply, felt comfortable enough with one another to anticipate the next face to make, the next pose to take. And as silly as it might seem to certain people, I believe they were building something with their selfies and their shared lip balms and their excitable chatter that some people can't understand or simply refuse to.

All of us can learn from that youthful defiance, that rejection of judgement. If we want to really make the best use of our time here, we must grant ourselves the permission to be loud and silly, and joyful and unconcerned in our displays of friendship and shared adoration. Judgement will come just as surely as time will pass, and there may be a time ahead when you can't laugh uncontrollably with your friends all in one place, when photos and videos are all you have, and you'll wish more than anything that you let yourself take even more, filling the vault with joy, laughter and evidence of the loving community you made together.

A few years ago, a photo of the plaque on a memorial bench went viral on social media and it still crops up on my feeds now and then. The plaque read: 'For my life-long best friend Judy, from Janice. We were girls together.' A simple, shattering, beautiful set of words that still moves me to tears if I see it when I'm tired or hormonal or even just a little bit hungover. Most memorial plaques are from children to parents or from spouse to spouse, but if you look hard and often enough, you'll find that it's not at all uncommon to find them from friends. There are the men at the cricket club marking a place for a lost member and friend, a young woman memorialising the place where she and her best friend would sit after school, a younger sister who deeply misses the big sister who was her first friend and best enemy.

These memorials show us how enduring friendships can be, how great and notable their absence is. Your friends can love you for the whole of your life, and so it matters a lot that you romanticise your time with them and take good care of the connections. They can be the loves of your life as truly and deeply as any partner or spouse can. They can offer you an abundance of attention and affection. They can challenge you and keep you honest, inviting you to grow as a person and change in all the best ways, overcoming fears and self-imposed limits. They can support you in raising your children, building your career, grieving deep losses, addressing injustice, helping to dismantle and rebuild as many versions of your life as you need until you arrive where you're meant to be and where you can most authentically thrive. They can tell you when you're wrong without attacking your character or tearing you down. They can challenge you when you're scared to go beyond what you know and what is familiar. They can hold your hands across the table of a shared favourite restaurant, let you fall asleep on their shoulder in the cab home after a long night out, be your good morning and your good night. They can be your first call in panic and pain, and in joy and triumph. You can greet them at the airport with an embarrassing sign and a huge bunch of flowers. They can arrive out of the blue after years of not making any new friends, changing what you believe you knew about love and acceptance and kindness. They can be the blueprint for how you know you deserve to be loved, the yardstick for what you will and will not accept. They can be everything if we let them, if we do our part.

WAYS TO ROMANTICISE YOUR FRIENDSHIPS

Throw the dinner party!
You know the ones – those long, indulgent dinners that you've seen people having in old French films, the ones where you stick long candles in empty wine bottles and let them burn down as you talk late into the night, until there's wax all over the table and there's barely any light left in the room. You can play scratchy records you got for pennies at the car boot sale, wear glamorous thrifted clothes, cook an eccentric recipe from a 1970s' cookbook and blow through an entire roll of black and white film. You can do this because it's a fun and novel way to make memories, to create a playful space in a harsh world and live there a while without judgement.

Take them out. Out out
Tell your friend a time, a place and how much to dress up. Treat that friend with the focused fascination that

so much of the time we reserve for romantic partners or strangers we meet on apps. Ask them questions and really listen to their answers. Ask about their childhood, what they're hoping for from the future, what scares them, what makes them feel brave, what smells remind them of their grandparents, what last made them cry with laughter. Pick up the whole bill at the end if you're able to do so, especially if you know that they're a person who rarely gets treated.

Reach out

Perhaps think of a friend that you've not spoken to in a while, someone you've drifted apart from a little but haven't had a falling out with. Tell them you hope they're doing well and that you think about them fondly. Even if it doesn't fully reignite the friendship, it's a nice way to send loveliness out into the universe and invite some back in return.

Get writing

Write long love notes and letters to your friends. Send them in the post, hide them around their flat or just put them directly into their hands. Tell them they're funny, beautiful, kind. Write them promises and poems and pretty phrases. Tell them how excited you are for your

future together, the things about them that you most love, most treasure. Write IOUs for hugs, slices of cake, days in bed watching movies and eating takeaway food. Write on personalised stationary, a Post-it or just on the back of old receipts – wherever. Just write.

Practise gratitude for the friends you can see often and try not to take them for granted

I'm lucky enough to live with my best friend and because I know it is unlikely to be forever, I am grateful for each day that she's the one who bears witness to my life, who I share domestic duties with, who I stay up late laughing with. If you're currently in the same city as your friends, the same university halls, the same house – say thank you to the world for that and try to make the most of it. Life changes in so many exciting and wonderful ways, but it can also put physical distance between us and our best friends. Enjoy it while it's happening.

Organise a book swap with a friend or a group of friends

Let them give you their copy of something they absolutely adore while you give them your copy of something you absolutely adore. Not only is it cheaper and less wasteful than buying your own copy of a book you may or may not like, it brings you together on something and lets you learn more about what lights one another up. Then, once you've finished reading, you can make an occasion out of the swap back, going out for a coffee and a slice of cake or a drink down the pub, where you can tell each other your thoughts and findings on what you read.

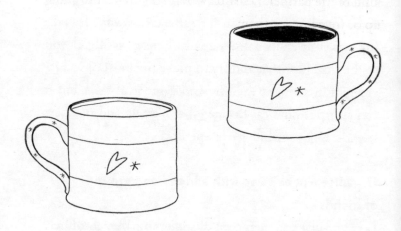

Don't let yourself talk about your friendships as though they're consolation relationships

If your date to the party or the wedding is your friend and not your partner, don't make a self-deprecating joke about it. Show them off! Be glad you don't have to worry about an impending breakup ruining all the amazing photos you take together. They're not there because you couldn't bag a proper date, they're there because you love them and you want to share them with the whole world. Dance, eat cake and introduce them to people with the same detail and pride as you would if they were any other kind of life partner. Don't play down their effort to show up or your love for them.

Here are some journal prompts and exercises to help you discover – and cultivate – the romance in your friendships:

Write a letter to a friend who lives a long way away from you. Include five things that you love about them.

....

....

....

....

....

....

....

....

....

....

....

The ways that I can best show up for my friends is by . . .

....

....

....

....

....

....

....

Five key lessons my friendships have taught
me are . . .

....

....

....

....

....

The main ways I can keep my long-distance friendships healthy and ongoing is . . .

....

....

....

....

....

....

Each week, I'd like to make a friend feel special and
seen. Here are some ways I could do this . . .

....

....

....

....

....

....

My best friend/s is/are . . .

....

....

....

....

....

....

....

My best memory/memories with them would be . . .

....

....

....

....

....

....

....

This World Is Yours: The Joys of Solo Travel

Romanticising your life can occur in the smaller gestures – noticing the smell of baking bread as you walk to work in the early morning, for example, or exchanging smiles freely and without any particular reason. It can also be done on a grander and more daring scale, such as leaving the country and travelling alone, or even just taking a day trip to the coast by yourself despite worries of judgemental looks or moments of loneliness. Solo travel can be one of the most liberating, expansive, joy-giving experiences. It can feel brutally and earthshakingly terrifying, or minorly uncomfortable, or none of the above. It can take you far away from home for months at a time, or just a few dozen miles down the motorway for twenty-four hours.

People often assume that because I've travelled frequently alone, both for my travel job or simply to escape to somewhere new, solo travelling must come naturally to me, that I must be inclined towards it. This could not be further from the truth. Growing up, I was constantly anxious about separation, panicking about being abandoned, getting lost or being left alone. Even in my early twenties, I'd get easily flustered by cancelled trains or changes in my journeys, planning frantically and exhaustively for every possible eventuality of any trip that I had to take by myself. I imagined myself stranded in foreign airports, being mugged, losing my wallet or passport, getting lost and succumbing to anxiety and simply shattering into pieces.

What this came down to was an inner distrust: I didn't believe myself capable of handling things; I didn't have the kind of fundamental faith in myself that is necessary when it comes to moving through the world freely and boldly. And so, for most of my life, the idea of travelling anywhere by myself that wasn't for work or to the shops was genuinely unthinkable – laughable, even. If anyone had asked me about it, I would probably have said that it just didn't appeal to me, before swiftly changing the subject. But in fact, it did appeal to me, very much, but since I believed it was an impossible feat, I tried to put it out of my head. I told myself that although some people were able to do it, I was not. Maybe in some other life. Maybe if I was anyone else besides me.

I never meant to end up as a seasoned solo traveller is what I'm saying, and it's taken a lot of learning and making mistakes. In fact, the first time I boarded a plane alone it wasn't out of bravery, to challenge my anxiety, expand my horizons or try something new – but for the same reason I made a lot of mistakes in my early twenties: a crush on a guy. I was in my early twenties, and having a hard time. I was dissatisfied and depressed, struggling to find my footing or think clearly about my future without withering under the anxiety of it all. Unsure of who I was or what I wanted (and without the accrued wisdom to know just how normal that was at that age), I tethered myself and all my worries to a man I barely knew.

It seems silly now but at the time it made a perfect kind of sense. Perhaps it was that he was a little older than me, had a job, opinions about politics, had his life together in a reassuringly grown-up way. All this combined made him seem like a real person in the real world in a way that I felt I was only ever mimicking. Or perhaps I could sense that I liked him just a little bit more than he liked me, and saw this as a challenge that I could rise to meet – that in winning his affection I could win my life. Whatever it was, he quickly became all I thought about. This guy, whose name I now sometimes struggle to recall, was someone around whom I could orbit in a universe that felt otherwise cold and strange.

And so, we went on messaging back and forth for months,

me staying up later and later to keep up with his schedule, turning my sleeping pattern on its head to fit into his East Coast time zone. By the time he eventually asked if I wanted to come and stay with him in Boston for a week that summer, I was practically nocturnal. I said yes right away. I didn't think about the logistics, the costs or the distance, only about how things were finally coming together for me. It seemed like the fates were aligning; a sad and lonely year at last transforming into something extraordinary by the prospect of us being together in the same city.

I really believed that I would go on this trip and be made brave by it, healed of my low moods, my worries about the future, my uncertainties about myself and all my (entirely normal) twenty-one-year-old insecurities. We'd begin a great romance against the backdrop of New England, strolling along the Charles River hand in hand, playing darts in boisterous Irish pubs and just generally being adorable together. I was certain that a week in the same city would catalyse something between us, make it real and everlasting.

I spent my remaining student loan on a plane ticket to America and started counting down the days.

My week in Boston was a dream but not in the way that

I'd hoped. On the descent into Logan airport, I was so tense, so worried about making a perfect first impression that I didn't so much as glance out of the window. I couldn't describe what the city looked like from above in the evening twilight – if the buildings were lit up like so many stars in the sky or if you could see boats bobbing on the water – because I was too busy freshening up my makeup and nervously nibbling at the skin around my nails to spare a moment to look. There was a tense, almost poisonous apprehension inside of me where there should have been genuine excitement and anticipation.

The ingredients were there for me to treat this as an adventure and a break from my life back home, but instead of feeling excited and present, I felt out of sorts and disconnected. I couldn't relax because I was so laser focused on him, so worried about his perception of me, his judgement, his approval. I barely noticed the city around me, the city I'd wanted to visit since I was a little girl, burning through disc after disc of the Ally McBeal boxset with my mum every Sunday afternoon, imagining myself cheering in Fenway Park or picnicking among the immaculate flower beds in Boston Common. I hardly felt a thing when I sat on the lakeside bench under the willow tree where they filmed the iconic scene in Good Will Hunting when Robin Williams makes his famous speech to Matt Damon. (If I ask you about love, you'd probably quote me a sonnet. But you've never looked at a woman and been totally vulnerable. Known someone who can level you with her eyes.')

My anxiety was terrible. I ate too little and drank too much, waking up early every morning with my heart hammering, feeling either soothed by his arms around me or distressed to find his sleeping body turned away. When we walked through the city in the late afternoons, I was blind to the skyline and the cheery overspill outside the old pubs, the worn yet stately glamour of the city buildings, the sweet, lingering smell of the Dunkin Donuts that seemed to live on every single corner. When he went into the office during the day I did very little, sleeping late and then walking the same loop of his neighbourhood, all the while watching the clock and waiting for his return. I'd set off from his front steps only going as far as the metro station, barely ten minutes away before returning to his building and beginning the loop again.

On one particularly hot afternoon, he suggested that

I walk to the nearby lake and obediently I did. I sat on a bench by the water with my book open in my lap, trying and failing to read it. The words seemed to rearrange themselves on the page in front of me, becoming garbled nonsense, a language I couldn't understand. I put the book away and instead tried my hardest to notice, to use the mindfulness exercises I'd learned from a university counsellor I'd seen the previous winter. I did my best to breathe, to absorb the immediate world and connect to what was happening around me.

There were cheerful American families with maps and matching outfits, apple-cheeked toddlers in pushchairs messily eating ice cream while their mother chatted to them in sweet soothing tones, runners in tight Lycra puffing their way around and around the circumference of the lake. The silvery water lapped the shore near my feet, the trees danced in a barely there breeze while the sailboats bobbed.

It helped a little to do this, though I remained anxious, self-conscious and full of doubt. I was realising too late how little I knew about the man I was falling asleep with every night, how flimsy a reason he had been to fly so far. I hadn't gotten any further away from my problems –

I had, in fact, brought them with me. I felt disappointed and deflated, a party balloon leaking helium, dipping lower and lower, aimlessly drifting towards nothing.

My disappointment in myself was palpable and the shame of it was like a second skin that I wore all week long. I had no idea how to be there essentially alone, how to take control of the trip, accept that it had started on a false premise and would probably not end in eternal love, but make the best of the remainder of it, following my own whims and exploring on my own terms. I didn't feel brave enough, bold enough, good enough. I didn't feel like I had permission to try.

My week there ended how it was always going to end: a quick goodbye and a kiss at an airport drop-off zone, followed by conversations that grew shorter and shorter until he and I weren't in touch at all.

For a couple of years, the trip lingered in my memory as a shameful failure, an embarrassing attempt to be spontaneous and stretch my wings that had only clipped them further. I considered it hard proof that I was simply not cut out for grand adventure or solo travelling, which is an easy mind trap to fall into. Because when a first attempt at something goes a little awry, or we find ourselves hurt or embarrassed, we're quick to take it as evidence of some bigger personal deficit, proof that we shouldn't have tried in the first place, confirmation that our world was only meant to be so big and we should stop.

Thankfully, after a few years, I was able to look back at that trip to Boston with kinder and fairer eyes. In doing so, I found that even the most sharply painful memories had been worn smooth, and that what remained was something relatable and entirely understandable – a lost young woman simply trying her best to feel found, to feel happy, to feel loved. Instead of feeling scornful of twenty-one-year-old me, I only wanted to go back in time and greet her at Gatwick arrivals, jetlagged and puffy eyed from crying for most of the flight, to take the heavy bag from her shoulder, give her a great big hug, and tell her that things do and will get better. That this is not game over on adventure and bravery.

I forgave her, forgave the guy who never actually promised more than he'd delivered, forgave Boston itself – which couldn't be blamed for not working some miracle on my young and turbulent life – and forgave solo travelling. I realised that it *wasn't* closed off to me after all, that there was no further debt to pay or shameful mistake to make up for. I could use the experience as a learning curve. I could try and try again.

So, I did, and this time I started smaller.

I planned a short writing trip outside of London – something I'd seen other writers do and had always wanted to try. My destination was the seaside city of Brighton. My reasoning was as follows:

1. It was very close to where I lived, barely a two-hour journey door to door.

2. It was somewhere I'd visited dozens of times in my life – as a kid paddling in the sea in my knickers and vest, as a teenager sneaking into sticky floored clubs, as an adult for nights out and to visit friends and family.

3. I adore the sea and have long been convinced that the fresh, salty air has the power to make me happier and healthier than I've ever been, reviving me as though I'm a sickly Victorian lady who has been to a coastal resort to clear up a bout of flu and hysteria.

I told myself that I'd tap into new sources of creativity

and achieve fame and acclaim off the back of the writing I did there. I was certain that I'd love it.

And I did – for about the first two hours following my arrival. By the next morning, however, I was feeling almost as alone as I had that week in Boston, even though the time that had passed between these two trips felt infinite and utterly transformative. I knew that I wasn't the same me as I'd been years earlier when I'd taken that transatlantic flight – scared and depressed and so unsure of myself that I'd been willing to outsource my entire sense of worth to an almost total stranger – and so I couldn't quite work out why I felt so lonely, so weighed down by embarrassment and self-consciousness. I'd worked so hard and for so long to be able to do this, to take myself on a small holiday, rent a flat near the seafront where I could write freely and live slowly for a few days. I'd been able to picture it so clearly before I came: me walking down cobbled streets, footloose and fancy-free, following the trail of inspiration wherever it took me. I'd write in cosy cafes, skim stones on the sea, take exhilarating dips in the freezing cold water and then reward myself with a glass of red wine and an enormous pie in front of a roaring pub fire. But now it was here and time to make it happen, I suddenly felt wildly out of place – a fish in a music video, a dog in a corporate job, a knock-knock joke in a eulogy.

My anxious mind told me to stay inside and hide, endure the burning FOMO and only emerge once a day to buy a sad microwave meal before retreating back to the flat in shame. Resisting that instruction was one of the tougher things I've done, but I managed it. I took a shower, dressed myself in some cosy clothes and gave myself a simple objective: *get some fresh air, buy a coffee and just see how it feels to exist in the outside world for a while.* I put my noise-cancelling headphones on, chose the most empowering, energising, courage-inducing song that exists ('Break My Stride' by Matthew Wilder, in case you were wondering) and walked out of the front door of the flat.

For the first hour of my mission, nothing much changed in my internal landscape. I remained fixated by my own singularity, scanning the area for couples and families and groups of friends that I could compare myself to. In the second hour, though, the fixation started to wane. My cheeks were red from the cold and the fast walking had energised me. I got another coffee, then chased it with a seasonally inappropriate ice lolly from the corner shop and wandered slowly along the beach eating it.

For a while, I stood very still at the edge of the water, trying to regulate my breathing, to notice what there was to notice – the salt foam smell of the sea, the distant whoosh of fairground rides and children laughing from the pier, the cold wind that whipped my hair all around my face, the sharp calls of the seagulls above. I didn't feel amazing but I did feel much better than I had. Though this doubt and anxiety was not quite what I'd expected when I'd booked the trip, I had to accept that it was what was happening, knowing that resisting it would only plant it more deeply. There was nothing for it besides this acceptance – sitting with what was uncomfortable until it passed. I kept on walking, feeling more and more courageous and spontaneous with each step, and by the time I got back to the flat later that afternoon I was excited again, happily moseying in with a tote bag full of second-hand books I was well aware that I'd struggle to carry back to London.

The rest of the trip went much the same way, joy and anxiety arriving hand in hand, some tricky mornings followed by calmer afternoons, restful evenings that weren't ever totally ruined if I felt a little strange or lonely or nervous or fretful. I had feelings and I treated them with practical kindness instead of dismissal, and though my anxiety never fully deserted me, I stopped demanding that it did.

Predictably, the next trip I took was a little bit easier, the one after that easier still. I went to Edinburgh in late November and took walks through sleepy Leith, had long lunches alone by the castle with a book, unhurriedly strolled through Christmas markets. I went to Brighton again the next spring and took brisk morning runs along the seafront, exchanging good morning smiles with elderly couples wandering hand in hand, I ate donuts on the pier and went on last minute dates with locals. I went to South Wales in the late summer, wild swimming and hikes up big hills followed by greasy hamburgers from vans at the side of the road. I made a list of places I'd like to see in my lifetime, both in the country where I live and outside of it. It no longer felt like a shot in the dark, but rather like a plan and a genuine intention. Like a prayer I repeated I *can*, I *want to*, I *will*.

In spring of last year, I travelled alone to the Greek island of Hydra. It was a four-hour flight from Heathrow to Athens, a sixty-minute metro ride to Piraeus port and then a further two hours by ferry. When the boat docked at Hydra in the early evening, I'd been travelling for fourteen hours, my back and shoulders aching from lugging my huge backpack from one country to another. The sun hung low in the sky and the streetlights were just coming on along the port; waiters were setting down candles on tables and grocers were closing their shop fronts for the evening. I'd had two large Greek lagers on the final leg of the journey and when I picked up my bag from the ferry's luggage hold and went to swing it up and onto my shoulders I very almost toppled clean off the deck and into the sea.

I chose Hydra in part because of the writer and musician Leonard Cohen, who had lived there on the island in the 1960s, when he was in his twenties and still almost a decade away from releasing his first album, writing and playing music, looking out of windows and falling in love. I've always felt a fondness for Leonard Cohen and his low, smoky voice and lovelorn lyrics, but it wasn't until a particularly painful breakup with an artist when I was in my mid-twenties that he became a musician and writer I truly loved, and, for a time, even genuinely depended on.

The last time I saw the artist was the previous November, when I'd travelled to Italy to spend a week with him. He'd moved there a few months after we'd met, going to make art and see beauty and take his next step. I went there only for him, hoping that closing the distance would help bring us back together and bridge a gap between us that by then was bigger than the miles on a map. It didn't work. By December we were through and I was crying on my parents' sofa, a position I maintained for weeks on end, growing gradually stronger on a diet of parental encouragement, episodes of Bob's Burgers and my dad's hearty vegetarian cooking.

During this period, I listened almost exclusively to The

Songs of Leonard Cohen, his debut album, with a frequency that bordered on obsession. I went to bed and listened to it with my head under the covers. I took myself on walks in the weak winter sun and played it, stomping around the countryside for no other reason than because moving my body felt marginally better than not moving my body. I put it on in the kitchen as my appetite returned and I was able to find joy in food again, and in the car on the way back to London when I finally felt ready to be without the support of my parents, when wallowing was no longer an option, when life was inviting me to return, to participate, to try it all again.

At first, I thought of my ex while I was listening to the album. The song 'Hey, That's No Way to Say Goodbye' had come on shuffle just as my flight home was taking off – it was the last time we'd see one another for almost two years, though I hadn't known that then – and I'd privately decided that it would be our song, his and mine. The lyrics about morning kisses, far-off cities, forests, distances and goodbyes felt like they were written for us, and so for a long time after we broke up, I couldn't listen to it at all, and would skip it whenever it came on. But eventually, I did listen and I found that even as it made me cry, I really, really loved it, loved it as much as I've ever loved any song, and I felt better for letting it play through. It felt like I was taking the song back, line by line, for myself. The memories were mine, the songs, the places we'd been and the places we'd talked about going. I took it all back: our plans would be my plans, the cities would be mine, the forests and all the distances, too. Spring was coming and I was tired of goodbye. I made my plan and booked my flights to Athens. I would go to Hydra by myself.

It wasn't only because of Leonard Cohen that I wanted to go, because his writing about it had become so important to me or because he had seemed to find a kind of magic there that I wanted some of for myself. I wanted to go because I wanted to go, and after years of getting on planes to follow men I was ready to expand my own personal horizon, following some internal call towards joy, pleasure, discovery. In a letter to his mother, Cohen wrote of Hydra: 'I live on a hill and life has been going on here exactly the same for hundreds of years . . .' As a writer without inspiration and a romantic without romance, I couldn't think of anything better than a week or so of living this kind of life. I could follow where others had walked, could get up early and write, could love the heat, could swim in the sea in between chapters. I could find my way back to myself, be who I wanted to be, live as I pleased.

As in Cohen's days, there are still no cars on the island and even though the house I'd rented was a fifteen-minute uphill walk, I decided to decline the fifteen-euro aid of a local man and his local donkey and tackle it by myself. I was stiff and tired from travelling, and I wanted some fresh air and time alone. Halfway up the hill, I regretted everything and when I eventually arrived at the front door of the old villa, I was dripping with sweat and so out of breath that I swear I could see cartoon stars spinning around my head.

The place I'd chosen was too big for one person – two bedrooms, two bathrooms, a balcony and a sprawling terrace – but it was cheaper than a hotel room or a small apartment down in the port. It felt lovely and lived in, the front step worn into a groove by the many pairs feet that had been stepping in and out of the house for as many decades as it had stood here. Inside, there were doilies draped over every available surface and vague smells: cooking, incense and those citrussy candles you burn to keep mosquitos away. The kitchen cupboards were painted a shamrock green, each tilting slightly off rusted hinges, full of odd, unmatching glassware, crockery, board games, old VHS and cassette tapes, bug spray and perfume bottles so old that they barely held any scent. A large gold gilt-framed painting of Jesus hung over the kitchen bins.

Upstairs, I dropped my bag in the corner of the master bedroom and opened the shutters, just in time to watch the last few moments of the sun setting across the water, radioactive orange melting into a grey-blue sea.

I turned on the lamps in the bedroom, took a quick and freezing cold shower (I was too tired to attempt to work out how the electric water heater worked) and changed into clean jeans and a T-shirt. I packed for a dinner alone, throwing a couple of books into a tote bag along with an unopened bottle of water, a camera, a notebook and pen, and my portable charger. On the walk back down the hill into town I took great care, watching both for uneven ground and dark heaps of dry donkey poo that I'd spotted on my trek up. There were no lights besides the weak beam from my phone torch, a few lit windows and the yellow glow from a new moon hanging overhead. It wasn't much but it was enough.

I was too hungry to explore far and so chose a little

taverna at the near side of the square, ordering an enormous bowl of pasta and a glass of white wine almost immediately after taking my seat. I ate, read and eavesdropped on conversations happening around me, understanding some, not understanding others and not minding either way. My shoulders, tense after the journey, gradually dropped and relaxed.

After I'd finished eating, I ordered a second glass of wine, which the owner of the taverna brought out to me himself. He said hello and introduced himself. My book was sitting open but ignored on the table, a fat tabby cat sleeping soundly in my lap. He looked at the lone bowl, the single wine glass, the empty chair on the other side of the small table and asked if I was there on the island

alone. I told him I was, trusting him easily with information I would usually keep to myself, for my own safety telling strangers who asked that I was travelling with friends or a partner or had family nearby. He considered this a moment, then asked if I was lonely by myself. I didn't answer, and instead just gestured to the view and the wine and the sleeping cat as if to say, *What more could a person want? What more could any of us need?*

This kind of deflection has become a bit of a habit on solo trips, as I often struggle to explain my experiences of solo travel to the many people who ask me about it. How to tell a stranger that yes, there are indeed many moments of loneliness when I travel by myself but that it isn't the kind of loneliness I can easily name, and nothing like the loneliness I've felt at home. How to explain that it isn't a loneliness that makes demands of me or alters the fundamental beauty of a place – it can, in fact, even sharpen it. It isn't a loneliness that feels related to isolation or yearning, not a feeling that makes me wish things were different. It's more like a shadow, a feeling that is free to come along with me wherever I go, sitting quietly at my heels or across the table or beside me on the bus while I go about the business of experiencing a new place, being in the world with nothing besides my own company. It tells me the facts – that I am alone – but it accuses me of nothing. It is a messenger, a deliverer of information that I am free to engage with or ignore.

Travelling alone is not always easy, not even if you feel born to do it or have done it dozens and dozens of times. It can be terrifying, mortifying and both physically and mentally depleting. For many of us, it involves challenging our anxiety and learning to override panic, doing the very thing that our nervous systems are screaming at us not to do. For some people, taking a trip abroad alone is a no-brainer – *Of course, why not? Where's my passport?* etc. – whereas for others, it takes an Olympian effort to even consider it. When you're anxious in this way your brain will resist your every plea for it to chill out, get on board, bend even slightly towards some new approach or experience. And when this happens it's important to remember that it isn't resisting because it's a mean bastard of an organ that wants your life to be small and miserable and empty of adventure and romance. It's doing it because that is what it has evolved to do – e.g. keep you safe within the limits of what it knows and what is familiar. Out of this protective instinct, it will replay the same set of stories about your limitations, repeat the same false but familiar lines about what you're capable of and what is simply not meant for you. It will conjure an image of you alone in a restaurant or a bar or on the beach, discomfort humming all the way to the ends of your fingertips, the hot glare of other people's judgement like a rash over every inch of exposed skin. It will scold you for wasting your money, for ever believing yourself worth the trouble, the time, the expense of a whole trip just for you. It will resist and tug you backwards towards safety and familiarity.

It isn't easy but I promise that you can disagree with your brain's assessment of what is safe and what is allowed. Even if it scares the living daylights out of you, you can book the trip, check the expiry date on your passport, pack your bag and go. It will get easier, too. With experience and practice comes ease and confidence. You'll grow familiar with the admin and the emotional sensations of taking these trips alone, and less will surprise you or catch you off guard. You'll no longer reach immediately for panic and terror when there's a hitch in your plans. When a train or a plane is delayed, you'll find the beauty in the unexpected free time. You'll buy yourself a plate of oysters and a glass of champagne in the airport at 9am or

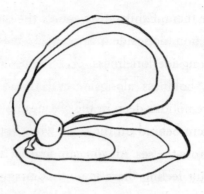

drag your bag back to the beach and take a nap against it. When the last ferry ticket sells out before you can reach the front of the queue, you'll allow yourself one irritated sigh before booking a seat on the next one and taking it as an instruction to explore where you are a little longer, take the time you have and do something nice with it. And when you feel lonely or anxious, you will allow those feelings to approach, arrive and then pass without overidentifying with them or building some tragic and permanent story.

When you travel alone all your fears and difficult feelings come with you, and I've learned that there's no real way around this. But I've learned too that it can be a gift to have all these feelings and that we don't need to explain or overanalyse them. Exhilaration can exist alongside anxiety, satisfaction alongside a hunger for more, peaceful solitude alongside loneliness, pride alongside self-consciousness, boldness alongside uncertainty. You can't stash your emotions deep in the overhead compartment or leave them behind on the dock while you board the ferry and cross the sea. All you can do is to trust that for each difficult feeling there is an accompanying action. If you need to talk, you can use a phrasebook or Google translate to say 'hello' and 'how are you?' and 'my name is'. If you're lonely you can call someone you love and tell them all about it. If you feel uncomfortable and self-conscious you can take your body walking through city streets, running along the coastline, swimming in cold, lifegiving water.

When I go somewhere alone it is always far more than a journey of buses and boats, planes and trains. It's the sum of all the years of trying, of feeling deep discomfort, of not quite making it, of trying again. It's been a journey of slowly dismantling the deeply held beliefs about what is possible for me and what I'm capable of doing. I've had to take leaps and exist for extended periods of time within discomfort and fear. It has often not been the fun, blissful escape that it would have appeared to be on social media, but it has always, always been worth it.

Nowadays, I leave London alone without a second thought – the proximity and cost of travel making the Kent and Sussex coast my most visited destination: a day in Whitstable, Broadstairs, Margate, Brighton, Dungeness. I savour the planning, the variety of carefully selected objects that I'll bring with me. On a cold winter morning, a second pair of socks and a torch, a portable charger and room for whatever sandwich is cheapest at the train station. Sometimes I'm impulsive – a towel and a good book shoved hurriedly into a bag at 6am on a scorching summer morning. Other times, I prepare meticulously the day before, filling my backpack until the seams strain, packing carefully cut summer fruits, a decadent salad, a flask of iced lemonade, a bulky film camera, a sachet of deep conditioner that I can comb through my hair after the harsh salt water, two or sometimes three books, a notebook and pen, a plastic cup, a bottle of sparkling wine I've been saving for a special day.

As I leave home, I relish the fact that there's nobody to discourage me, to tell me that one book is probably enough, that I should leave the notebook behind because it will go untouched as it always does, that the wine will be too heavy and I should just buy something at the supermarket. When I travel alone my opinion is the only one to be considered, my desire the only compass to follow. I can set an alarm for 5am or sleep in and delay leaving until the afternoon, and nobody can grumble or argue, hurry me up or ask me to wait. With nobody else to distract me, I can focus more acutely on the things I see, the things I hear, the things that happen to me: the gorgeous blur of lush green countryside through the train window, the golden summer sun spilling onto my face, the same tender, pink burn in the middle of my back that I get every summer, the one place on my body that I'm unable to reach when applying my own sun cream. A seasonal legacy – there, then not there, then there again.

Travelling alone has taught me patience and pleasure and the place where the two meet, merging to become a unique third thing. It has made me better at travelling with other people, too. I savour their company because I know how it feels to be without it. I recall a moment when I was away and I missed them, and I'm able to practise gratitude that I am not missing them any longer. Doing this has made me calm when there's a delay or a change of plan, or I encounter someone else's fleeting bad mood or frustration. I can tolerate uncertainty in ways I never could when I was younger, before travelling alone was a major part of my life.

While promoting the 2022 film The Banshees of Inisherin, Colin Farrell said that he ran the length and breadth of the Irish islands where they were filming. He talked poignantly about the connection you can find to nature when you embrace your 'aloneness'. This kind of aloneness is what I go in search of when I take these trips, either for a day or for longer. You can get closer to the world alone, and it can get closer to you.

Last year I went back to Boston. My flight from Gatwick was due to depart at 10am. I arrived at the airport early, drank strong coffee and browsed beautiful designer clothes that I'd need to sell a major organ to ever buy. As the plane was taxiing, I made small talk with the woman beside me. We talked about the cancelled trains that morning, her nightmare multi-bus journey to the airport, the kind airline employee who declined to charge me for excess baggage despite my luggage being 4kg over the limit. She asked about my plans in Boston – if I was visiting friends, where I was going to stay, whether I was travelling for work or leisure. She asked if I'd ever been to Boston before and I quickly tried to decide whether to tell her the whole sorry tale or a white lie, explaining my decades-old *Ally McBeal* fantasy and the unknown city that awaited me at the other end of the journey. Instead, I told her the short version of the truth: I went once a long time ago and now I'm going back.

This time, I did look out of the window as the plane touched down. It was midday and overcast, the white-grey sky and low-hanging fog making the city seem colourless and flat. Someone in the row ahead joked that we might as well be touching back down in London. I beamed out of the window, a little tipsy from the G&T I'd ordered, sleep deprived in a way that made me giddy and giggly. I said goodbye to my seat mate as we were separated into different queues at passport control, realising too late that I'd never asked for her name, silently hoping for us both to have the trip that we wanted. As I waited for my suitcase to appear at baggage claim, I felt a great relief that there was no near-stranger waiting to meet me at arrivals. I could grab my bag and go, skipping the traffic and the small talk and making my own way, something twenty-one-year-old me would have thought herself incapable of.

In the cab, I watched the city rush towards me, the buildings towering up into the misty grey sky. I'm here, I thought, at last. I was thousands of miles away from home, in a city that for so long represented rejection and failure and fear. I was alone, excited, nervous, but exactly where I felt that I was meant to be. I've got this, I told myself. It's going to be great.

And it was great – it really, really was – though it was far from perfect. Things went sideways and plans changed as they will always change. It rained heavily the only day I left my umbrella at the hotel and my shoes and jeans were soaked by a speeding lorry. For the first twenty-four hours, I failed to find anything resembling a grocery store and had to eat packets of crisps, dense bodega sandwiches and overpriced room service meals. After getting ready for a date, I got a text from them telling me they had to work late and would need to reschedule. One afternoon, I felt overcome by such a deep homesickness and sense of isolation that I cried for forty minutes in the park, walking around with tears streaming down my cheeks until I was stopped very abruptly by a man dressed head to toe in red and gold velour asking if I would help him film a TikTok. And help him I did, crying all the while, and when he walked away I started laughing so hard at the ridiculousness of the encounter that I forgot I had been feeling sad at all. It turns out that no feeling is permanent when you're travelling, just as no feeling is permanent when you're at home.

Moments of connection are almost constantly available when you're away alone if you'll only pay attention. One evening, a friend of mine got me on the guest list for a Father John Misty show down by the water. At the box office, I found they'd set aside two tickets. Just as I was about to tell them I only needed the one, I overheard a young woman at the next booth along asking if there were any tickets left to buy. I went over and offered her my

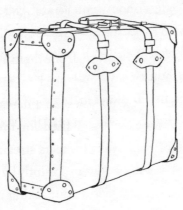

spare for free. Our seats were side by side and so we sat and chatted as we waited for the gig to start, talking about what had brought us each here. I told her I was travelling partly for work, partly to settle a score with the city. She told me she had just moved there that week for a new job. When the band came on, we smiled at each other, two strangers singing along side by side in the dark.

And another. Passing through airport security on my way home, I caught eyes with the woman I'd sat beside on the journey out. We were on the same plane home, both there hours before the gate opened, and she asked if I'd like to get dinner. I didn't hesitate in saying yes. We sat together in an airport restaurant, drinking wine and telling one another about our trips. It was so lovely we missed the gate announcement and were the last two people to board the plane. It was only after I had collected my bag, wheeled it through customs and was heading for my train home that I realised that again, we hadn't exchanged names. It didn't matter. She was a stranger on her own journey and I was just glad that we had met.

MORE TIPS FOR SOLO TRAVELLING

Allow room for the less glamorous elements

The impossibly long ticket queue at the train station, the mosquitos that seem hellbent on sucking every drop of blood from your body, the deeply undignified miming act you have to do at the pharmacy after eating questionable seafood at a truck stop – these are all a part of what it means to go far away from home, to take an adventure, to explore this world. Try to laugh about them, either in the moment or as soon as possible after, letting them become funny stories and, in doing so, removing any power they may have to ruin your day or derail your trip.

Accept that some of your plans will change

A flight or a train journey will be delayed, a flight connection will be missed, a hostel will be flooded when you arrive, a taxi will drop you off miles from where you asked to go, your favourite sunglasses will get swept into the sea or an unseasonal rain storm will blow into town on the day of the fun, sexy boat trip you've booked. And it will just be life being life! You can allow yourself to feel the frustration and the anxiety that come with these scuppered plans while also refusing to read too much into them, such as them representing your own cursed bad luck. Things sometimes go one way, but they can also go the other way too. Make a new plan and try to keep it going.

Seek out the beauty in the more mundane moments

Solo travelling is not only about impromptu all-night raves, Michelin-star meals, spicy summer romances, perfect city skylines, hotel upgrades and unbelievable golden sunsets and sunrises. No – it's also the rainy forecast that leaves you with little to do but trail around a damp and unfamiliar place in an unflattering anorak. It's the local family you see in matching knitted jumpers at the landmark who ask you to take their photo and ask you if you want your photo taken too. It's the joyful noises drifting up from the destination beach wedding you're watching from your plastic chair at the bar, the quiet moment of journalling in a cafe while you wait for your bus to arrive, the view of the morning through the window on a sleeper train while everyone around you is unconscious. These moments don't need to be stricken from the record or assigned a lesser spot in memory.

There can be great beauty in quiet, reflective days or dull mornings stocking up on groceries for your journey from one exciting place to the next. These things tell you that you are there, you are brave, you are damn well doing the thing.

Go, just to go

You may well make an epic emotional breakthrough and find yourself, but also you may not. And if you don't, it won't mean the solo trip wasn't worthwhile. Sometimes a holiday is just a holiday – a leisurely break from your normal surroundings and your usual routines. Joy, rest and pleasure can be their own rewards. You certainly haven't 'failed' at taking a solo trip if you don't return with an entirely new worldview or philosophy. Most people don't! Going away alone is far more often about the quiet courage of trying something new than it is about total spiritual and emotional reinvention. If you're seeing more of this world, having joyful experiences (even if they exist alongside some anxiety) and giving yourself a break then you're doing more than enough. You're doing brilliantly.

Keep a journal or a photo diary

This doesn't need to be anything official – just an open and ongoing note on your phone where you jot down memories or certain details of your days can help enhance the trip in many ways while also preserving your memories. When you're travelling with others you can rely on them to help you remember what happened and when, but when you're flying solo that responsibility falls to you. Record-keeping, therefore, is very important and even if it's a little slapdash, it can be a great way to hold onto the details, leaving you more to look back on in the future, to learn from and enjoy when you're back home.

Journalling or diary keeping is also a brilliant therapeutic exercise when you're somewhere new and unknown, keeping you busy and brave and allowing you a space to plan or to work through any difficult feelings. Carrying

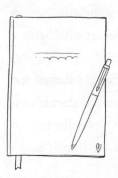

a biro and my battered journal has given me something to do during countless meals, on trains and when delayed at an airport. Similarly, taking an old point-and-shoot film camera with me has gotten me out and about on days when I've felt particularly anxious and insular. I tell myself that I just need to snap five pictures and then if I'm still feeling terrible, I can return home and hide. Almost always, that impulse passes after I've picked up my camera and gone out in search of beautiful sights.

Make time to talk to the people you come across
More often than not, you'll find that this can be an adventure all on its own. Travelling is, after all, an opportunity to expand your perspective in every direction and gather new information about the world. Engaging with the people you meet along the way is one of the easiest ways to make this happen, learning from them and perhaps giving them a bit of what you've learned. You can get so much from striking up a conversation with the other guests at your hotel, the woman who is also dining alone or the person sitting beside you on the plane, the train or the ferry. Take a deep breath, smile and start with hello.

Take steps to be safe and stay alert but trust yourself too
One of the biggest reasons that I wanted to start travelling by myself was to move beyond my own limits and build on what I believed I was capable of. Nerves and a

degree of sensible awareness are great – especially if you're travelling alone as a woman – but try to avoid moving through each new place with a sense of immediate unease or hypervigilance. This will only make it harder to spot the lovely, romantic details of the place: the subtle interactions happening in a community, the smells of local restaurants and food stalls, the flowers growing up between the paving stones, the friendly faces. And it's alright if it takes practice to get there, to learn to relax without totally dropping your guard. When I first travelled by myself, I was brittle with anxiety for the first few days. I felt watched and judged, and worried constantly I was going to do something to make myself a target for crime or violence. But with patience and time this feeling passed, to be replaced by a more measured set of emotions. I'm now far better at separating intuition and good sense from anxiety and pure fear, and in doing so have managed to take a deeper enjoyment from my travels, and a deeper appreciation of my instincts.

Romanticise coming back home again too

Travel can be an escape and a chance for an amazing adventure, but for most of us it will be a temporary departure. We have homes and roots and jobs, responsibilities and families, things that will always call us back from even the furthest lands. I've come to learn that this doesn't mean we have to dread that return flight or let the sadness at coming back poison our last few days in an incredible place. Make space for disappointment and a kind of mourning period at the end of an adventure but try not to sink too far into it. Instead, remind yourself of everything that you're excited to be returning to: your friends and your family, the familiarity of the life that you've worked to build, the postman, the man in the corner shop, a bath, a fridge full of food, all your own clothes hanging patiently in the wardrobe, the full body relaxation you can only really achieve in your own home.

Don't shop like a doomsday prepper

As an anxious traveller with ADHD and sensory issues, I do appreciate that some purchases can be game-changing and worth the cost (noise-cancelling headphones for long flights, the very best portable charger, packing cubes and pill organisers, etc.), but the idea that you need to kit yourself out with dozens of shiny new things to make a trip worthwhile is flawed. You absolutely don't need to buy more than you can comfortably afford and poorly made items panic bought on Amazon are not what will make the difference between a great trip and a disastrous one. Instead, see what you already have and what you can borrow from friends. This way there's less waste and more money left over to do the things you really want to do when

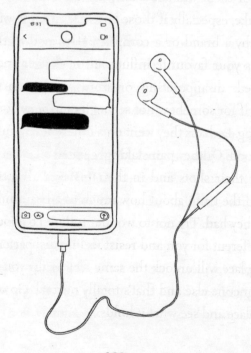

you're away: eating and drinking, going to galleries or gigs, buying souvenirs or paying for experiences or tours.

Don't worry if your trip doesn't always look Instagrammable

A lot of travel content on social media is heavily edited and carefully curated. No disrespect to travel bloggers, vloggers or content creators, but it's a simple fact that many of them will show only a certain side to the trips they take, especially if those trips are in some way sponsored by a brand or a company. If you go to the same spot as your favourite influencer or vlogger and find it crowded, disappointing or uninspiring, don't blame yourself for somehow not seeing its magic or for getting it wrong. Perhaps they went on a different day, in a different mood. Or they painstakingly edited all other tourists out of their shots and in their Instagram caption they fudged the truth about how much of a beautiful, serene time they had. Try not to wonder too much about why it felt different for you and resist feeling disheartened. Not every place will unlock the same feeling for you as it did for someone else and that's totally normal. Go on to the next place and see what it holds.

It's impossible to leave all your feelings, attachments, worries and problems behind you when you travel – so don't try

A trip can be wonderful even if there are complex emotions, low moments, real anxiety or a level of uncertainty that never quite leaves you. Trying to predict exactly how you'll feel and exactly how a trip will go is an attempt at control, which can only ever really end in your misery and disappointment. So, instead of trying to map out every feeling or reaction, and pinpoint which moments should and will be your favourites, how about approaching the whole thing with curiosity and an intention of discovery?

Stay open to detours

Some of the most brilliant fun I've had while solo travelling has happened on the parts of trips that I'd predicted ahead of time would be the most mundane – layovers or rainy mornings working in cafes or a quiet dinner alone near the hotel. A boring breakfast was transformed when I was joined by an old Italian man who asked me about the book I was reading, told me all about the very best places in the city to eat and set me up on a date later that day with his (very handsome) grandson. A sedate walking tour that was rained off after twenty minutes ended as a bar crawl that lasted until the early hours and a power failure in a Greek restaurant meant that me and six other diners were hustled upstairs to eat together at the owner's own kitchen table. You can't predict these things but you can stay open to them.

Here are some journal prompts that help me to work through anxiety or uncertainty about solo travel, so I can refocus my desires and grow my courage:

List some worries you have about solo travelling and the practical steps you could take to overcome them:

....

....

....

....

If you had a wobbly moment while solo travelling you could cheer yourself up by . . .

....

....

....

Your reasons for wanting to try solo travelling are . . .

....

....

....

....

Travelling solo, you would be totally free to . . .

....

....

....

....

Going on holiday alone would be a great chance to grow and expand yourself in which ways?

....

....

....

....

Your ideal solo trip would include these five things . . .

....

....

....

....

....

You could comfortably pass the time eating or drinking alone in a restaurant by . . .

....

....

....

....

....

....

....

The places you most want to visit are . . .

....

....

....

....

....

....

What mantra would you like to live by when travelling alone? (TIP: You have full permission to be as cheesy as you like here. For example, I tell myself 'Future you is so proud right now' and 'You don't have to do this perfectly, you just have to do it').

....

....

....

....

A Note on Toxic Positivity and Privilege

There has been backlash to the term 'romanticising your life' since it began to bloom and spread on social media. As more people were experimenting with it and deciding what it meant to them, critics were quick to suggest that it is a practice only possible for the most privileged of us, requiring the kind of money, time and access that most ordinary people don't have. I have to disagree.

Certainly it's true that not everything can be romanticised. There are some days that are just terrible and some situations that are simply beyond salvage, which must be endured and lived through, rather than brightened, sweetened or solved. Romanticising your life can be a force for all kinds of growth and good, and I do believe that it can help us expand our curiosity, build our resilience and add a great quantity of joy to our lives – but what it *can't* do is unmake a very difficult situation. It can't untwist that terrible anxiety that comes while waiting for bad news or weathering rejection, dealing with illness or loss or heartbreak. It is not a greater force than grief or poverty, betrayal or abandonment. It's not even bigger than a bout of mild food poisoning.

What romanticising *can* be, sometimes, on a few of those inevitably hard days and in certain draining situations, is a glimmer of good and vital light. It can be a whisper from the dark that reminds you that loveliness, fun and play are still real, and still meant for you, even if you can't access them for a while. It can be an invitation to take a timeout during a crisis so you can pause and catch your breath. It can be a reminder to be soft with yourself when your instinct is to beat yourself up, a nudge to seek out some small moment of pleasure, laughter, rest and beauty among moments of pain and upheaval. It can soften a landscape, even if it can't always change it.

I was recently in the bathroom of a pub in East London. The walls of the toilet stalls were scrawled with graffiti and I took a little time to read it. It was the usual stuff – encouraging and funny notes, drunken scribbles, song lyrics in bold Sharpie lines, some angry critique of exes, names joined together inside hearts, initials thickly carved with house keys. Messages written by dozens of people as they used this loo, total strangers talking to one another across time. As I was leaving the cubicle, I noticed a quote written neatly and compactly in red felt pen right at the top of the stall door. I looked closer. It read 'argue with reality, welcome to hell'. I repeated the phrase to myself as I washed my hands. It seemed so apt and something I could do with remembering. *Argue with reality, welcome to hell.*

Arguing with reality is what toxic positivity is and what romanticising your life is not. Toxic positivity is shouting down or forcibly ignoring anything that isn't totally cheery, upbeat or easy-going. It's labelling people as negative for struggling or feeling unhappy, dissatisfied and not immediately able to find the bright side of a situation. It's telling someone who is in great emotional pain that they just need to try harder if they want feel better, that they should stop focusing on the bad stuff and instead think more about the good stuff.

Toxic positivity is a kind of suppression. It requires denial – and lots of it. In reality, life can – and does – get very hard. Feelings of anger, sadness, uncertainty, loneliness, jealousy, confusion and exhaustion will appear for all of us, and that's totally normal. It might happen in isolation or as a reaction to grief, loss, injustice, illness, disability. Experiencing these emotions, or any emotions, that aren't strictly 'positive' is not a failing of any kind, it's just the reality of being a person on earth. We can't shame these feelings out of the picture and pretend they're unnatural, while insisting that positive thoughts, mindfulness, meditation or gratitude is the only valid or proper response. Things can and will get hard for each of us, and it's not negative, gloomy or unromantic to acknowledge that. We all will, at times, struggle and feel complex feelings, and we'll have to face them and work through them patiently and with help. Most, if not all of us, will experience derailing mental and physical health challenges during our lives. For many, it's the norm. Pain and distress like this can naturally interrupt a journey of romantic living, or at least change how you're able go about your search.

When I was nineteen years old, I dealt with my first very bad bout of depression. I was away at university and I didn't yet know how to ask for help, didn't even know that I was allowed to. I fell behind on my coursework, sleeping through most of each day and then staying up staring at the ceiling through the nights. The things I'd enjoyed so much just a few months before – spending time with new friends, dancing in crowded bars to cheesy pop songs, writing short stories, swimming at the leisure centre, studying film and literature – all lost their shine, one by one. The colour drained from the world and my desire to be a part of things went with it. Had you asked me then, in that state, to tell you what might help romanticise my life a little, I'd have laughed bitterly and then probably cried. I felt beyond help then, genuinely too ill most days to get up or function. I was further than the reach of herbal tea in a nice pot, the almost-sweet smell of old bookshops or a walk at sunrise. I was ill and I was tired, and what I needed was proper treatment and ongoing care.

Though it seemed at the time like I'd never start to feel better, I of course did. Over time, and with the support of professionals and loved ones, I began to lift out of the worst of it, and the world slowly but surely opened up for me. I no longer had to argue myself out of bed or into the shower, no longer had to rely on meals that took under forty seconds to prepare. I could walk and eat, cook and move, and even laugh again.

With the help of a campus counsellor, I found ways to cope with moments of sharp anxiety or despair, learning to tap into and utilise my senses when I felt overwhelmed or anxious. I focused on what I could see, feel, hear and smell, training myself away from some unknowable and frightening future and back into the safety and certainty of the present moment. I lowered my gaze and narrowed my perspective until each day felt manageable, then okay, then good. When my mood was low, I would think only of the next five or ten minutes.

I walked every single day. I walked and I noticed, and I tried to remain alert not to those imagined and exaggerated dangers that might be lurking ahead, but to the beauty, peace and joy that was right there in that moment, all around me, waiting to be discovered. In this way, I grew an awareness that has stayed with me ever since, one that I'm able to tap into whenever I most need or want to. Though I didn't name it as such at the time, I see now that I was romanticising my life during this period of recovery. I was taking the spaces that felt most broken and stripped away and filling them in again. I found daily practices that kept me rooted in the present, connecting me with pleasure, community and peace, even in the smallest of ways.

Despite all the time that has passed since I slipped down into that first terrible darkness of depression, I still remember how it felt to fall and how it felt to come back towards the light. Living through that time taught me that although it can be tempting to think that it's possible to crack the code of life and to figure out how to permanently live in a romantic and happy state, it isn't. Almost no one can exist easily and jubilantly forever, adoring the world, marvelling at the sunrise, feeling perfectly content as they cut into their carefully arranged stack of pancakes. That's simply not how it works. Human beings are complex animals and even the most 'well-lived' life involves ups and downs, grieving and making mistakes, hurting, being hurt. We don't begin at the beginning, work hard in just the right ways, figure out the correct attitude to have and then move permanently into the camp of people who are fine and happy forever. Things go wrong every day for people who are good and kind and work hard. They go entirely tits up after years and years of the tits going the correct and predictable way. One day, you can feel anointed by angels and then the next, you can find yourself fired or dumped or trying frantically to wipe bird shit out of your hair as the bus you've been waiting on for half an hour zooms right by. One moment, your world can feel sensibly contained on all sides and the next, something can happen that takes the air out of your lungs. Nobody is protected from that, not by positive thinking, not by romanticising the moment, not by anything.

Life is made up of unavoidably difficult moments and romanticising your life isn't a way of trying to avoid those, but rather of finding joy in the margins, holding tight to hope and restoring yourself to better emotional health after pain and struggle. It can be a way to start practising real gratitude when things *are* going well, when there is beauty in the picture, and making the effort to notice it and trying to lean inwards instead of away. It can be one of the things that you can use to help you to claw your way up out of darkness – but it can also just be a way to brighten up a boring Tuesday.

Romanticising your life can also be a way to disrupt a bad pattern and get out of a particular rut. If you find yourself feeling burned out by work, doing too much for others and not enough for yourself, having the exact same day one after the next after the next, then it can be a way to help launch (or gently nudge) yourself towards joy, rest and loveliness. Sometimes, it's enough to try to adjust your perspective or routine and see if the air feels a little lighter as a result. It can help, even in a small way, to carve out intentional time to be a bit indulgent – to take a brand-new book to the cafe, to mute a stressful conversation, to make yourself a lunch-time picnic, to pamper your body head to toe.

What romanticising is *not* is an invitation to scoff at other people or find ways to condescend to them if they choose a different approach. Making your life more romantic is a practice that looks different for each one of us, and someone's decision to try it or not try it is none of our business. We must resist the urge to label anyone who doesn't want to live the same way as us as unromantic, cowardly, lacking something or missing the point. If a person is happy with the way they're moving through the world – or even if they're not but haven't asked for your opinion or input – then you need to leave them to it, wish them well and reserve your judgement. Romanticising your life is something entirely personal, a practice you adopt for your own enrichment and joy, not to position yourself as higher or better or more enlightened than anyone else who has chosen to do things in their own way. It's one approach, sure, but it's certainly not the only way to live and to make this life and this time on earth worthwhile.

It's also very important to bear in mind that what is possible for one person may not be possible for another. Just as our needs and tastes are different, so are our abilities, limits and options. Parents have less free time than child-free individuals and likely far less cash. People who live in poverty and without disposable income will not be able to take off at the drop of a hat to go on a day trip or a last-minute holiday. Disabled and chronically ill people are affected by the shameful lack of accessibility in many public spaces, private business and travel destinations. Certain countries or cities on one person's bucket list may be hostile and downright dangerous to queer people, trans people, people of colour, those of a certain faith.

Therefore, when considering these lifestyle choices and pursuits, it matters that we're able to be honest with ourselves about what our privilege allows and makes space for. Time, money, accessibility, energy, a seat at the table – these are not as abundant as many of us believe. Consistent leisure hours in the mornings or evenings may be scarce for many workers. White people may take for granted how much leeway we are given to behave as we please in public spaces, unafraid of intervention by racist bystanders or police.

All of this we can bear in mind when making our suggestions or encouraging others to follow our example directly. The world is not a place of unlimited freedoms for all, and though romance is for anyone and everyone who wants it, it's not a one-size-fits all endeavour. Can our view of this practice therefore expand to include helping to build a more romantic world for others as well as ourselves? Can we see the romance inherent in being a part of a community, of standing shoulder to shoulder with others and fighting with them to push for a better future?

I think we can. I believe that each of us can chase joy and build romance into our personal lives while also listening actively and learning how to help improve the circumstances of others. When we pursue this way of living with zero self-reflection, we can end up in performance mode, making it into Instagram or TikTok fodder that

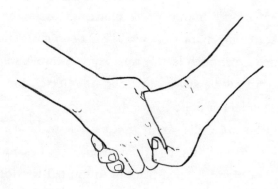

does nothing for the quality of our lives or the deepening of peace. Instead, let's go on making memories, seeking pleasure and romance and heart-exploding joy, and let's do so while also considering how best to use whatever privilege we possess to do some good in the time we have.

Main Character Energy

Some days invite you to be the main character.

You might feel it as a particular charge in the air, as an energy of abundance, adventure or courage that wasn't there the day before, and you'll feel called to stand up a little taller, to move through the world as though you are at its heart, at its helm, the lead in the film, the protagonist of the novel, the star of the show. This might come after a lull or a funk, a breakup that knocked your confidence, a loss or rejection that took you out of the moment and away from yourself. It might be an internal call away from self-diminishing and ruminating towards fun, play, exuberance and excess.

Whatever it is, these days ask to be answered. They invite you to go deep into your wardrobe and choose your very best things: your most loved dress, an as-yet unworn thrifted jumpsuit, the shimmering sequinned jacket or the bright yellow hair ribbon – anything that makes you feel radiant, brave, beautiful and lovely. These days invite you to walk with purpose out of your front door and into the world, living from that moment on in the film or the fantasy world of your choosing. You'll put in your headphones and play a favourite soundtrack while you walk through your neighbourhood, allowing the traffic, the frustrated commuters and the dogs peeing against traffic cones to become a part of the opening sequence, the first notes of a beautiful song.

Maybe the character will be one of vixen or spy, heroine or disruptor, and you'll wear the reddest red lipstick shade, an added dab of perfume or aftershave, a beret over pin curls, a crisp white shirt, an impenetrably dark pair of sunglasses. You'll smile at the best-looking person on the train through the window just as it pulls away. You'll walk into the hotel bar as though you've been staying there for six months, as though you own the place. You'll order a martini to your exact specifications and sigh with satis-

faction when you take the first sip, as though a director somewhere has told you to really give it your all. You'll adopt a mysterious expression, a twinkle in your eye or a mischievous smile – as though you know something about this world that nobody else does.

Or perhaps this isn't the film that you're in. Maybe instead of the dim hotel bar it's a sprawling park, a meadow or the pebbly beach of a quaint seaside town, and the director calls action as you're lying on a huge blanket reading a book or listening to music with a decadent picnic spread around you – fizzy wine overspilling the crystal glass that you wrapped carefully and brought all the way here, nestled in your basket beside chocolate strawberries, freshly baked bread and homemade pesto hummus.

Or maybe you're not in a film at all but instead the protagonist of a play where the stage is your kitchen and the cast are your most loved friends, and all the action takes place around your second-hand dining table with its one wonky leg and scratches and scuffs. Perhaps in this play there's a dinner party in your honour, for no other reason than because, and you will make speeches, your friends will make speeches, and you will eat and drink and laugh with one another until the candles have burned into waxy puddles on the table and it feels like everyone else in the world has gone to sleep. Maybe you'll hold yourself as though you were in a novel or a poem, the fictional character you've always loved or an entirely new character altogether.

WAYS TO EMBRACE AND EMBODY YOUR INNER MAIN CHARACTER . . .

Head to the movies

Sometimes escaping into a fictional universe is the perfect way to access some more inner magic and inspiration. If the real world feels like it's dragging you in its wake then there's no harm in ditching it for a few hours, choosing a movie that reminds you of what kind of life you'd like to live and then taking notes. Go where the characters are bold, where love is abundant, where there's bravery and joy, challenge and triumph. And when the film is finished, go on living in that world for the rest of the day. My favourites are *Amélie*, *Pretty Woman*, *Breakfast at Tiffany's*. Cliché? Couldn't care less. I'm too busy being the star.

Throw some main character outfits together

Take that stagnant, 'I have no clothes and nothing fits me' feeling and prove it wrong. Dig out all of your clothes and put together some new outfits – both for upcoming events and for plans you've been daydreaming about, plans you plan to make happen. A solo day at the beach, a date in a sultry speakeasy, a morning sketching in the museum, a night dancing with your best friends. It's a hopeful exercise, this one, and one that can reconnect you to your personal sense of style and image.

Go to where the action is

Even if there's a little flutter of anxiety or hesitation, do it anyway. See how it feels to sit alone right at the bar in an expensive hotel, to take out your sketching pencils at the café table, to park yourself right in front of the most beautiful painting in the gallery, to confidently try on a pair of sunglasses you'd have to sell your soul to buy, to squeeze yourself into the crowd at a gig for a band you've never heard of. Experiment.

Make the soundtrack

Music is the perfect bridge between desire and action, filling in for whatever confidence that you're yet to build. Create a playlist that will get you into whatever headspace you're trying to access, whatever character you're trying to emulate. I like listening to film soundtracks from beginning to end as I walk around, even if I'm just shopping for cereal and toilet roll or going to the post office. Make a soundtrack of every single song that makes you feel like the protagonist.

There are so many ways to be the main character, but also so many excuses not to bother. Embarrassment, shame, other people's judgement – take your pick. All forces that seem powerful and inarguable but in fact . . . aren't, and are in fact just noise, a frequency that you can choose to tune into or learn to ignore.

Being the main character is an idea that has often found itself on the receiving end of scorn or rolled eyes since it found its way into the public imagination and the internet. But to be the main character is not to treat other people as though they're inferior, a supporting cast that exist only to do and say what you want them to do and say. To be the main character is simply to adopt a different attitude towards yourself, the space you allow yourself to occupy and the whims you dare to follow. It's not narcissism or arrogance to do this, not a blinkered world view that diminishes or hurts other people. It's quite appropriate to find yourself important, to decide that your life matters and that the way that you live will not be decided by sneering strangers.

The truth is that there's nothing you can do on earth that won't cause someone, somewhere to roll their eyes and begin talking about how that this is the *real* problem with society. You can't escape this, so why not give up trying? Why not instead let yourself do the fun, indulgent thing that hurts nobody? Why not emancipate yourself from your own judgement and the judgment of others by letting yourself feel playful, important, cherished and chosen?

You'll do it. Not always, but sometimes. You'll do it because you can, because you want to, because it's fun, because – why not? You'll do it because you know in your truest heart that other people's judgement or sneering has no currency at all and, in the end, life is simply too short to say no and not bother. Be the main character, even if just for an hour, an afternoon, a weekend. If the world is going to spin around anyway, then why not, now and again, let it spin around you?

Afterword

In 1975, Joan Didion made a commencement address to graduating students at UC Riverside in California. She told those assembled not to focus on progressing in the world or making it better, but instead to focus on living in it. To do more than go through life as though it was a punishment. She asked them, quite simply and quite brilliantly, to live in it. To take advantage of every moment they're given.

I've returned to her speech again and again over the years, coming back to it whenever I need a reminder that life is only so long, and that bravery and kindness and joy are always available to me. When it's time to decide whether to do something scary or courageous or new, whether to demonstrate love openly or to put hate to rest and release myself from anger, whether to make a part of my life bigger or keep it small – I read those words. I ask: How can I really live in the world today? How can I seize at least one of today's many moments?

And the answer is always in the action, the answering of a call that comes both from all around and from deep inside.

Life really is only so long, so why not the wildflowers in every room, why not the walk in the rain, why not the afternoon feeding ducks, why not the sunrise, the sunset, why not the ice cream with all the sauces and sprinkles, why not all the love you can muster, why not all the things as often as you can have them?

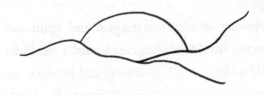

Acknowledgements

With thanks to my parents, Julia and Ray, for all of their invaluable support. To Archie, Lottie and Cal for the same. To Sean, who has greeted all of my growling with endless patience and humour. To my editor Carina Bryan for all of her enthusiasm and skill. To Michael Caine. To my grandparents. To Jess and Luke. To Stinky. To Seymour and Martine. To Bingo. To Issy, Liv, Millie, Molly (and Mandy, whoever she is). To Jonny. To Emma. To Em. To anyone who has read this far. To the hopeful and the sensitive and the open-hearted. Thank you, so much, to you all.

About the Author

Beth McColl is a London-based freelance writer, advice columnist, author, podcaster and public speaker creating written and audio content about mental health, sex, dating, travel and popular culture. She's written for *Dazed Digital*, *ELLE*, *Vice*, *Metro*, *Refinery29*, and *Glamour*.

Her first book *How to Come Alive Again* – a guide on how to navigate your mental health – was published in 2019.

Credits

Orion Spring would like to thank everyone at Orion who worked on the publication of *Romanticise Your Life*.

Editor
Carina Bryan

Copy-editor
Liz Marvin

Proofreader
Elise See Tai

Editorial Management
Jane Hughes
Charlie Panayiotou
Lucy Bilton
Claire Boyle

Audio
Paul Stark
Jake Alderson
Georgina Cutler

Contracts
Dan Herron
Ellie Bowker
Alyx Hurst

Design
Nick Shah
Joanna Ridley
Helen Ewing

239